From Wrongs to Gay Rights

Cruelty and Change for LGBT People in an Uncertain World

Dear Eric,
It's a pleasure to know you and to work with you. Keep up the good work!

Blessings,
Colin

COLIN STEWART, EDITOR

P.C. Haddiwiggle Publishing Company
21 Marseille
Laguna Niguel, Calif.

ISBN: 978-0-9830206-2-2
LCCN: 2013901921

Printed in the United States of America

INTRODUCTION

In a world where 76+ countries still have laws against homosexuality, a same-sex kiss can lead to a prison sentence or even execution. That's the setting for this book about "cruelty and change for LGBT people in an uncertain world." The topic is huge, so the book can provide no more than a few glimpses into the joys and pains of modern-day lesbian, gay, bisexual and transgender people.

Much of the content of the book comes from the Erasing 76 Crimes blog (http://76crimes.com), which focuses on the human toll of 76-to-78-plus countries' anti-gay laws and the struggle of those countries' LGBT people seeking justice and equality. The quest of sexual minorities for dignity and fair treatment is much the same, whether they are called homosexual, gay, lesbian, bisexual, transgender, LGBT, LGBTI (including intersex people formerly called hermaphrodites), LGBTIQ (including people who describe themselves as queer or questioning), or other labels.

Authors include LGBT activists in Cameroon, Uganda, the United Kingdom, the United States and Zimbabwe.

Proceeds from the sale of the book will be used to support the Erasing 76 Crimes blog and the work of activists seeking a better life for sexual minorities worldwide.

Contents

PERSONAL STORIES

GLIMPSES

SOURCES

FROM WRONGS TO GAY RIGHTS

OVERVIEWS

FROM WRONGS TO GAY RIGHTS

Victories, setbacks, close calls: 2012 in review

By COLIN STEWART

The idea that people should be thrown in jail for loving the wrong people fell out of favor last year in a few countries, even as the battle for basic human rights for lesbian, gay, bisexual and transgender (LGBT) people raged from Singapore to Moscow and from sub-Saharan Africa to the Caribbean.

During the year, advocates of LGBT rights achieved some victories, suffered some setbacks, and narrowly avoided a few potentially heart-wrenching defeats.

Among people of faith who joined the fray, the loudest voices spoke of condemnation for LGBT people, not love, often bolstered by a stubborn insistence that people can choose whom they will be attracted to sexually. In contrast, religious leaders who emphasize the commandment to love your neighbor were

Miss Gay pageant winner Thapelo Makutle, was killed in South Africa in 2012, apparently because of sexual orientation.

often distracted by other issues, or their calls for reconciliation were drowned out.

For many people in the Americas and Western Europe, disputes over distant countries' anti-homosexuality laws were overshadowed by joy or worries about the growing acceptance of same-sex marriage, which is now legal in 11 countries, in parts of Mexico and Brazil, and in nine states in the United States.

Also in the background were repeated instances of unpunished murders of LGBT people and the ongoing spread of HIV infection among gay men who are typically denied health services in the 76-plus countries with laws against homosexual activity.

PROGRESS

During 2012, India and Malawi — two of those 76-plus countries — took steps to repeal or suspend enforcement of their discriminatory laws. Another four countries moved in that direction.

Malawi President Joyce Banda is seeking repeal of the country's anti-gay law.

In India, the supreme court let stand a lower-court ruling that overturned a British colonial-era law providing life sentences for homosexual activity.

A similar court proceeding was under way in Singapore.

In Africa, Malawi suspended enforcement of a British-originated law providing 14-year prison sentences for homosexual acts.

In early 2013 in South America, Guyana was in the midst of a formal governmental evaluation of whether to repeal the law calling for life sentences for male-male sex acts.

In the Caribbean, the government in Trinidad and Tobago was pushing to outlaw discrimination against LGBT people, including repeal of the anti-LGBT law that allowed for prison sentences of up to 25 years for sexual activity.

FROM WRONGS TO GAY RIGHTS

In Europe, a court case was under way that sought to overturn a law calling for five-year prison sentences for male-male sexual activity in Northern Cyprus, which is overseen by Turkey. The Turkish Republic of Northern Cyprus is the only part of Europe with a law against homosexual behavior, including continental border-straddling Turkey itself.

SETBACKS

The prime minister of Jamaica called for parliamentary action to repeal a law providing for 10-year prison sentences for men who have sex with men, but she backed off when it became clear that a majority of the current parliament would vote against any such a change.

Portia Simpson-Miller, prime minister of Jamaica

In Russia, where a law against same-sex activity was dropped in 1993, anti-homosexuality forces launched two new offensives.

Ten regional governments in Russia, including St. Petersburg, enacted laws banning "homosexual propaganda" where children might be present. A proposal to extend that ban nationwide was put forward in 2012 and approved overwhelmingly in January 2013 in a first reading by the lower house of the Russian parliament, or Duma. It was sent for further study by a parliamentary committee.

In practice, such laws could prohibit any public discussion of homosexuality or advocacy of gay rights, depending on how local courts rule. Gay-friendly entertainers Madonna and Lady Gaga both ran afoul of those laws when they advocated equal rights during concerts in St. Petersburg.

In the Ukraine parliament, a similar proposal won preliminary approval in October. Similar bans were adopted in several cities in Moldava and were proposed by not enacted in Latvia, Lithuania and Hungary.

A further offensive by anti-homosexuality activists was a Russian-backed resolution at the U.N. Human Rights Council in support of

Madonna was accused of violating St. Petersburg's law against "gay propaganda" when she spoke up for gay rights during a concert there.

"traditional values," which can be used to deny human rights to women and to LGBT people.

The council adopted the resolution by a vote of 25-15, in part because its wording was appealing — it called for a study of how to apply "traditional values while promoting and protecting human rights and upholding human dignity."

In practice, the promotion of "traditional values" often endangers human rights. Russian authorities said they were defending traditional values when they prohibited gay pride marches in Moscow for 100 years and put the band Pussy Riot on trial for protesting in a Moscow cathedral.

ON THE BRINK

Early in 2013, three countries with anti-gay laws were poised to enact even more repressive measures.

Politicians advocating an anti-homosexuality agenda in Zimbabwe, Nigeria and Uganda were preparing to complete action on measures that they pushed in 2012.

In Zimbabwe, gay sex was already punishable by a prison sentence of up to one year, but anti-LGBT politicians didn't think that was enough, so they added anti-gay language to the country's proposed new constitution. The new document included provisions from the ruling Zanu PF party that condemned both homosexual behavior and same-sex marriage. A nationwide referendum on the proposed new constitution was planned for the spring.

In Nigeria, anti-gay politicians were also pushing for tougher laws. They were not satisfied with the 14-year prison sentences for homosexual activity that were already on the books outside the northern region where sharia law allows for execution of homosexuals.

A bill approved in preliminary forms by both houses of the Nigerian legislature would make same-sex marriage punishable by 14 years in prison for the couple and 10 years in prison for anyone who helped with the ceremony. The bill would also ban gay-rights organizations and provide a 10-year prison sentence for any public display of same-sex affection. Unless opponents of the law could mount an effective campaign against it, supporters predicted that a final version of the bill would pass early in 2013, after which President Goodluck Jonathan would either sign it or veto it.

In Uganda, 2012 saw the return of the world's most notorious anti-gay legislation, the "Kill the Gays" bill, which earned that label in 2009 because it would have imposed the death sentence on gays who repeatedly failed to remain celibate. The bill would outlaw LGBT support groups and would require parents, teachers, doctors and priests to report to police any suspected homosexual children, students, patients and parishioners.

Anti-LGBT politicians and conservative religious leaders pushed hard for passage of the Anti-Homosexuality Bill, even

Archbishop Desmond Tutu (Photo by Remy Steinegger/World Economic Forum via Wikimedia Commons)

though Uganda already had a harsh law, largely unenforced, that provided life sentences for homosexual activity.

More than a million people responded to the revival of the Uganda bill by signing online petitions against it. Former Archbishop Desmond Tutu of South Africa was among those calling for its defeat, but some other influential religious leaders who opposed the bill in the past mostly kept their opinions to themselves. In contrast to 2009, when the Vatican announced its opposition to the bill, the Pope focused on opposing same-sex marriage. In contrast to 2009, when best-selling author/preacher Rick Warren made a video calling for the bill's defeat, Warren only expressed his opposition in a 102-character message on Twitter.

The 2012 session of the Ugandan parliament ended with no action on the bill, but support for it remained strong. Most observers predicted that it would pass in 2013.

ONGOING REPRESSION

Separate from these legislative battles about gay rights, LGBT people in many nations face ongoing repression.

In Saudi Arabia, religious police continue their crackdown on homosexuals. A total of people 260 people were arrested and punished for homosexuality in a one-year period, according to one Saudi newspaper. Because media freedom is so limited there, the accuracy of that account cannot be verified.

In Iraq, since the departure of American troops, conservative militias have targeted sexual minorities. At least dozens, and perhaps hundreds, of LGBT people have been reported killed by militia in recent years without interference from police, and sometimes with police assistance.

In the central African nation of Cameroon, officials did not respond to a plea a dozen international human rights groups, including the United Nations human rights office, that they stop arresting and imprisoning people for being, or even just seeming, lesbian or gay. At the end of 2012, about eight people were incarcerated because of Cameroon's anti-homosexuality law and many more were awaiting trials that could lead to imprisonment.

In Iran, same-sex relationships are punishable by death, but sex-change surgeries are relatively easy to obtain and are covered by health insurance. As a result, people in Iran undergo more such surgeries than in any other country except Thailand. Estimates of the number of transgender Iranians range from 15,000 to 150,000.

FROM WRONGS TO GAY RIGHTS

Will 2013 be any better than 2012? Will there be fewer violations of LGBT people's human rights, fewer laws prohibiting specific types of love, fewer arrests, fewer imprisonments, fewer murders?

Conceivably. But for any of that to happen, many people would need a change of heart. Many politicians would need to protect minorities rather than oppress them. And many religious people would need to love their neighbors more and judge their neighbors less.

78+ countries with anti-homosexuality laws

Laws against homosexual activity are on the books in at least 78 countries.

The total is 82 if you include political entities such as Gaza/Palestine, the Turkish-controlled northern portion of Cyprus, and Indonesia, where two large provinces outlaw homosexual acts.

For the St. Paul's Foundation for International Reconciliation, which seeks the repeal of those laws, the number is 76, because its Spirit of 76 Worldwide program supports LGBT activists in many of those countries.

The International Lesbian, Gay, Bisexual, Trans and Intersex Association, or ILGA, lists the following 78 (plus 4) countries with criminal laws against sexual activity by lesbian, gay, bisexual, transgender or intersex people:

Europe
82 Northern Cyprus

FROM WRONGS TO GAY RIGHTS

Africa		
1 Algeria	15 Lesotho	26 Senegal
2 Angola	16 Liberia	27 Seychelles
3 Benin	17 Libya	28 Sierra Leone
4 Botswana	18 Malawi	29 Somalia
5 Burundi	(enforcement	30 South Sudan
6 Cameroon	suspended)	31 Sudan
7 Comoros	19 Mauritania	32 Swaziland
8 Egypt	20 Mauritius	33 Tanzania
9 Eritrea	21 Morocco	34 Togo
10 Ethiopia	22 Mozambique	35 Tunisia
11 Gambia	23 Namibia	36 Uganda
12 Ghana	24 Nigeria	37 Zambia
13 Guinea	25 Sao Tome	38 Zimbabwe
14 Kenya		

Asia and the Middle East	
39 Afghanistan	50 Pakistan
40 Bangladesh	51 Palestine/Gaza Strip
41 Bhutan	52 Qatar
42 Brunei	53 Saudi Arabia
43 Iran	54 Singapore (enforcement suspended)
44 Kuwait	55 Sri Lanka
45 Lebanon	56 Syria
46 Malaysia	57 Turkmenistan
47 Maldives	58 United Arab Emirates
48 Myanmar	59 Uzbekistan
49 Oman	60 Yemen

FROM WRONGS TO GAY RIGHTS

Two Asian/Middle Eastern countries are listed separately by the ILGA with a notation that the legal status of homosexual acts there is unclear or uncertain:

- In Iraq, there is no law against homosexual acts, but homophobic violence is unchecked and self-appointed sharia judges reportedly have imposed sentences for homosexual behavior.
- In India, enforcement of the law against homosexual activity has been suspended by court action.

Americas	
61 Antigua & Barbuda 62 Barbados 63 Belize 64 Dominica 65 Grenada 66 Guyana	67 Jamaica 68 St Kitts & Nevis 69 St Lucia 70 St Vincent & the Grenadines 71 Trinidad & Tobago

Oceania	
72 Cook Islands 73 Indonesia (Aceh Province and South Sumatra) 74 Kirbati 75 Nauru 76 Palau	77 Papua New Guinea 78 Samoa 79 Solomon Islands 80 Tonga 81 Tuvalu

Also worth mentioning but not on a list of countries with laws against homosexuality are:

- Russia, where 10 regions have laws that prohibit positive references to homosexuality in the presence of minors and a nationwide version of that law has passed a first reading in parliament (the Duma).
- Moldava, where several cities have enacted similar laws against "homosexual propaganda."
- Ukraine, which has given preliminary legislative approval to a similar proposal, but so far has not enacted it.

12 behind bars, 16 more awaiting trial on homosexuality charges

This list provides a snapshot of LGBT people in prison because of anti-homosexuality laws as of early January 2013. By the time it is published, some prisoners will have been released and others will be incarcerated.

By COLIN STEWART

As 2012 ended and 2013 began, the arrests of two gay-rights workers in Uganda brought to at least 12 the number of people worldwide who were imprisoned after being arrested or convicted of violating laws that punish those who are born gay, lesbian or bisexual. In addition, at least 16 other people are out on bail while awaiting trial for homosexuality.

The prison sentences imposed vary from one to five years — at the low end of punishments that are on the books in the 78-plus countries where homosexuality is currently illegal.

Listing 28 names is probably an extreme understatement of the number of people who are behind bars or awaiting trial on anti-homosexuality charges, but finding out about specific cases is difficult, especially in countries without a free press.

The lists below provide a narrow window into just one of many types of injustice affecting lesbian, gay, bisexual, transgender and intersex people, sometimes with fatal results.

The lists are dominated by Cameroon (seven in prison and 15 awaiting trial), with Nigeria and Uganda a distant second (two jailed in each country). All three of those countries have active news media in addition to repressive laws.

Just one man in Saudi Arabia (name unknown) is on the lists. No word has been received about his status since he was sentenced to five years in prison in 2010.

Jonas Singa Kumie and Franky Djome pose with their attorney, Alice Nkom, during the appeal of their five-year sentence in Cameroon.

Two men are listed as awaiting trial in Zimbabwe, while two other Zimbabwean men get a mention, although the facts of their case are in dispute.

Until New Year's week, no one in Uganda was on the lists, despite that country's deserved reputation for homophobia. Uganda's LGBT people confront stigma, rejection, extortion, exclusion from health care, and the possibility of passage of the notorious "Kill the Gays" bill. Now the police in Uganda have started making homosexuality-related arrests too.

12 people in prison

Nigerian law provides for sentences of up to 14 years for homosexual activity. In parts of northern Nigeria where sharia law applies, the death penalty can be applied for same-sex intercourse.

Dispute over prostitute's pay

1 and 2. Ifeanyi Chukwu Agah and Rabiu Benedict Yusuf
Two years in prison. Sentenced March 21, 2012.

Ifeanyi Chukwu Agah and Rabiu Benedict Yusuf were convicted of same-sex intercourse after police said Rabiu refused to pay Ifeanyi for his services as a prostitute. Rabiu asked for mercy on the grounds that he was married with six children, but the court rejected his plea.

Under sharia law, the death penalty can be imposed for homosexual activity in Saudi Arabia. Only one specific case has been recently reported, but that may be a gross understatement of what actually goes on without any publicity.

Lashed, then imprisoned

3. Name unknown
5 years in prison

In November 2010, a 27-year-old Saudi Arabian man was sentenced to 500 lashes and five years' imprisonment by a court in Jeddah for the criminal offence of homosexuality, among other charges, Amnesty International reported.

FROM WRONGS TO GAY RIGHTS

>>>>>>>>>>>>>>>> **CAMEROON** < <<<<<<<<<<<<<<<

Cameroonian law provides for sentences of up to five years for homosexual activity. As of the beginning of 2013, seven people were in prison in Cameroon on homosexuality charges.

Pursued by a mob

4 and 5. Jonas Singha Kumie and Franky Ndome (Djome)
5 years in prison

Jonas Singa Kumie and Franky Djome were in a group of three men who were arrested in July 2011 for homosexual acts. They were sentenced to five years in prison. They were

still incarcerated during the first week of 2013 — at the time of this head count — but in early January they won their appeal. On their release, they were pursued by an anti-gay mob, so they went into hiding. Back in 2011, the third man who was arrested with them paid a fine and was quickly released.

Subjected to anal exams

6, 7 and 8. Joseph Magloire Ombwa, Séraphin Ntsama and Nicolas Ntamack
In prison awaiting trial.

Joseph Magloire Ombwa, Séraphin Ntsama, and Nicolas Ntamack were among a group of four men arrested August 10, 2011, on homosexuality charges and subjected to anal examinations. They are still being held at the central prison in Yaoundé awaiting trial. In January 2012, along with Jonas Singa Kumie and Franky Djome,. they issued a New Year's message expressing thanks to their supporters for giving them reason to hope. Charges were dropped against Tiomela Lontsi (Emma Tiomela Lontsie), the fourth man arrested with them in

August 2011. Ntamack was released in mid-2012, but soon was re-arrested on new charges, so he and his two co-defendants are all in prison awaiting trial.

Seized by a mob

9. Cornelius Fonya
In prison awaiting trial.

Police in the coastal city of Limbe arrested Cornelius Fonya on Oct. 29 on homosexuality charges after a mob seized him and delivered him to the police station. He pleaded not guilty to the charges in a hearing on Nov. 7. His request for release on bail was denied. His lawyer says Fonya was arrested merely on the basis of the mob's accusation.

Sentenced to 12 months, served 15

10. Thomas Leba
In prison awaiting a decision on his appeal.

Amnesty International report: "In December 2012, Amnesty International delegates met and interviewed [Thomas Leba] at New Bell prison. .... Leba, 24, said he was arrested in Douala on 15 October 2011 and accused of being gay. The Court of First Instance in Douala found him guilty of homosexuality and sentenced him to one year's imprisonment. He appealed against his conviction and sentence. When Amnesty International met him in December he had already been in prison for 15 months but had not been released, apparently because he was awaiting a decision of the Court of Appeal."

>>>>>>>>>>>>>>>>>>> **UGANDA** < <<<<<<<<<<<<<<<

Ugandan law provides for life sentences for homosexual activity, though the law has rarely been enforced. Two young LGBT activists were arrested on homosexuality-related charges just before and just after New Year's Day 2013. They are included in this list because they were in custody during the first week of 2013.

Youth workers accused of 'promoting homosexuality'

11 and 12. Joseph Kawesi and Kabuye Najibu
Arrested; released, in hiding

Joseph Kawesi, the founder of the Youth on Rock Foundation, an organization that serves LGBT youth in Kampala, was arrested Dec. 31, 2012, on charges of homosexual activity and reportedly also of "promoting homosexuality," though that is not a criminal offense under Ugandan law. Kawesi was released on bail after a few days and went into hiding as he awaited word on whether charges against him would be pursued or dropped.

Kabuye Najibu was arrested Jan. 2 when he went to visit Kawesi in his cell at the police station where he is jailed. Najibu was reportedly accused of homosexual activity and "promoting homosexuality." Like Kawesi, he was released on bail, went into hiding and was awaiting word on what charges he would face.

16 more awaiting court action

>>>>>>>>>>>>>>>>> **CAMEROON** < <<<<<<<<<<<<<<<

A bribe triggered their release

1, 2. Stéphane Maliedji and Jean Jacques Eyock
Awaiting trial

Stéphane Maliedji and Jean Jacques Eyock of Cameroon, along with Australian citizen John Vasek, were arrested on March 26, 2010, on charges of violating Cameroon's anti-homosexuality laws. They were released after Vasek paid $2,500 to the police. The case is still pending, and Vasek has apparently left the country.

Arrest for looking 'too feminine'

3, 4 and 5. Aboubakar Siliki, Mbezele Yannick and Yntebeng Pascal
Awaiting trial.

FROM WRONGS TO GAY RIGHTS

Aboubakar Siliki and Mbezele Yannick were arrested in April 2011 on homosexuality charges after they went to the police station in Douala to try to resolve a dispute over finances. When Yntebeng Pascal arrived at the police station to discuss the situation, he too was arrested on homosexuality charges after police deemed him "too effeminate." The three men were detained for two days. They were then released awaiting trial.

Roger Jean-Claude Mbede shows the text message that led to his being sentenced to three years in prison for homosexuality.

Amnesty International prisoner of conscience

6. Roger Jean-Claude Mbede
Awaiting appeal of three-year sentence

FROM WRONGS TO GAY RIGHTS

Roger Jean-Claude Mbede is free temporarily for medical treatment after serving one year of a three-year prison sentence for homosexuality. He was arrested after sending a text message expressing his love to a man he thought was his friend. An Amnesty International prisoner of conscience, Mbede is appealing his sentence to the Supreme Court in Cameroon.

In an interview after he lost his previous appeal, Mbede worried about "going back to the dismal conditions that got me critically ill before I was temporarily released for medical reasons. I am not sure I can put up with the anti-gay attacks and harassment I underwent at the hands of fellow inmates and prison authorities."

Women arrested for living together

7 and 8. Esther Aboa Belinga and Martine Solange Abessolo
Awaiting trial

Three women in the city of Ambam were charged with lesbianism in February 2012. The first to be arrested were Esther Aboa Belinga and Martine Solange Abessolo, who were living together. They were detained for six days, then were released pending trial. Another woman was also charged after her husband accused her of being a lesbian —an accusation he made after Abessolo told warned him to keep his wife away from Belinga. Charges against the wife were later dropped.

Arrested after financial dispute

9. Samuel Gervais Akam
Awaiting trial

In the summer of 2012, an argument with a young man over money drew the attention of police to Samuel Gervais Akam, whom they arrested for homosexuality. He was held for months at the New Bell prison in Douala, during which time he fell ill and his wife died. In November 2012, he was released on bail to continue waiting for the trial to begin.

FROM WRONGS TO GAY RIGHTS

Village chief arrested

10. Louis Marcel Ijanja
Awaiting trial.

Louis Marcel Ijanja, a village chief, was arrested Sept. 3, 2010, in the coastal city of Kribi on charges of homosexuality. Eventually he was released from jail to await his trial.

Beaten and turned in to police by a mob

11, 12, 13 and 14. Gideon, Leonard, Elvis and R.
Awaiting trial

Four men identified as Gideon (or Gildeon), Leonard, Elvis (or Kelvin) and R (reportedly a minor) were arrested in December 2011 in the town of Kumba on homosexuality charges. They were denounced as homosexuals by an angry crowd, beaten, and turned over to police. They are still awaiting trial.

>>>>>>>>>>>>>>>> **ZIMBABWE** < <<<<<<<<<<<<<<

Zimbabwean law provides for sentences of up to one year for homosexual activity.

Anti-gay gang disrupts trial

15 and 16. Lionel Girezha and Ngonidzashe Chinya
Awaiting trial, perhaps in prison

Lionel Girezha, 27, and Ngonidzashe Chinya, 28, were arrested on Oct. 20, 2011, in the suburb of Mbare in Harare and charged with sodomy, Amnesty International reported. They were beaten before they were taken into police custody.

At their first trial, gang members harassed and threatened their lawyers, who successfully appealed to have the trial's location changed from Mbare.

According to one informal report, Girezha and Chinya have been released pending the start of a new trial.

Two more? Ability Chatira Mpofu and Blessing Chauke

Ability Chatira Mpofu and Blessing Chauke reportedly were arrested in September 2012 after police found that Chauke was wearing women's clothes and that the two men had gotten married.

But the activist group Gays and Lesbians of Zimbabwe said they did not know the two men, so they concluded that they were fictional creations of Zimbabwe's homophobic media.

Other injustices facing LGBT people

Of necessity, the lists above omit many types of injustices that confront LGBTI people worldwide. Here are a few of the omissions:

The lists do not include people who were executed in one of the seven countries where homosexual activity is a capital crime. (In Iran, three people were executed in 2011 for homosexual activities, according to Amnesty International.)

The lists do not include the dozens of gay men who reportedly have been killed by death squads in Iraq without any government interference and sometimes with help from police.

Matthew Shepard was killed in 1998, apparently because he was gay.

FROM WRONGS TO GAY RIGHTS

The lists do not include people killed by bigots because they are gay, such as Matthew Shepard in the United States in 1998, and an alleged 249 people in Peru during 2006-2010.

The lists do not include the many people who die of AIDS each year in countries where LGBT people are excluded from HIV prevention programs. Nor do they include the countless heterosexual women who die of AIDS after contracting HIV from their closeted gay or bisexual husband in countries where homosexuals are stigmatized.

The lists do not include lesbians and gays, such as Tyler Clementi of Rutgers University in the United States, who commit suicide because of the scorn they suffer or the unwarranted shame they feel because of who they are.

They do not include people killed because they are working for gay rights, such as Daniel Zamudio in Chile and Thapelo Makutle in South Africa in 2012 and perhaps David Kato in Uganda in 2011.

Last but not least, the lists do not include lesbian and bisexual women who suffer "corrective rapes" or sexual assaults because of their sexual orientation.

New activist network fighting AIDS and anti-LGBT laws

By COLIN STEWART

August 1, 2012 — Twenty-six LGBT activists traveled to Washington, D.C., two weeks ago, seeking to change a world where homosexuality is illegal in 76-plus countries.

Now that the International AIDS Conference is over, they are returning to their home countries, strengthened by the creation of a new faith-based network of activists with a common goal — guaranteeing the human rights and health of lesbians, gays, bisexuals and transgender people in those 76 homophobic societies.

"Against all odds they are working for inclusion and access to health services, church altars and the human rights for LGBT people in their countries. They are gay and straight, fresh young activists and older seasoned champions of truth, many of whom have created pioneering LGBT and HIV services for their home communities," said the Rev. Canon Albert Ogle, founder of the St. Paul's Foundation for International Reconciliation, which sponsored the Spirit of 76 Worldwide program that organized and paid for the gathering of activists.

FROM WRONGS TO GAY RIGHTS

Ugandan activist Danie Herbert meets with State Department staff

Three of the advocates came from Jamaica and Malawi, where, despite widespread homophobia, national leaders have publicly announced their intention to end anti-LGBT discrimination. These activists' task on returning home will be to build public support for those proposed changes.

The new Spirit of 76 Worldwide network includes two bishops, several priests and pastors, health workers, youth leaders, and many others whose faith leads them to confront the public health consequences of religion-based opposition to homosexuality.

"They had never been together as a group, but there was a deep bond of trust created immediately as they began to share their work and their stories," Ogle said.

"Some are Evangelicals while 40 percent are practicing Catholics. We have an agnostic who wanted to learn more about religion because he wanted to improve relations with the faith community in Singapore where he runs one of the few LGBT programs. We have a Muslim and a few African Anglicans whose churches had condemned them for working with criminals."

While in Washington, the group:

- Met with World Bank staff, who welcomed the activists' visit at a time when the bank is studying ways to prevent its programs from inadvertently harming sexual minorities in developing countries
- Met with State Department staff to nudge them to provide concrete support to back up Secretary of State Hillary

Clinton's declaration last year that "gay rights are human rights."

- Addressed gatherings focused on the faith community's impact on the AIDS epidemic, especially among men who have sex with men.
- Presented the documentary film "Call Me Kuchu" about religion, homophobia and the "Kill the Gays" bill in Uganda.
- Spoke at Washington area churches and took part in an interfaith service at the National Cathedral.
- Met with about a dozen conservative American lawmakers and their staff to tell them how the 76 countries' laws against homosexuality undercut U.S. anti-AIDS efforts abroad.

During their time in Washington, the activists also were trained in how to tell their stories most effectively and how to convince other people of faith of the need for dialogue and compassion, despite theological disagreements.

In addition, they set up a social media network that will allow the group to stay in touch with each other, offer suggestions, and provide encouragement in their common endeavors.

Shortly before leaving Washington, the activists shifted their focus to their next projects, which Spirit of 76 Worldwide organizers will present to potential donors who want to support faith-based initiatives against AIDS and for LGBT rights.

Among the proposals under consideration are plans for:

- Respectful interfaith dialogues in several countries, seeking to dispel homophobia by inviting clergy and lay people to discuss faith, AIDS and anti-homosexuality laws.
- Instructional videos about HIV, LGBT people and faith.
- An African website that would allow online discussions of issues such as AIDS, religion and homosexuality, even where a repressive regime forbids such discussions in public.

- Faith-based gay-straight alliances to combat AIDS, especially among marginalized sexual minorities.

The group has turned its past tribulations into future strengths, one African activist said.

"Like the Old Testament Job, all the people in the team have a heart-rending story to tell which scarred them. From tales of prejudice, personal attacks right down to the ills of 'corrective rape,' the people have had dark days behind them," he said.

"But like the sores all over Job's body, they have healed and are in the process of healing in a remarkable turn of events. What has not killed them has now made them hardened and determined to achieve their goals of decriminalization in their countries."

Growing support for same-sex marriage

Starting in the Netherlands in 2001, same-sex marriage now is officially recognized throughout 11 countries and in portions of three others. Elsewhere it is either not authorized or is formally prohibited. As this book went to print, France and the United Kingdom seemed close to approving marriage equality too.

The Netherlands (2001)

"Why should heterosexuals be able to fence off a part of civil law — marriage — and defend it as exclusively theirs? This 'separate but equal' status reminded me of apartheid in South Africa and Jim Crow in the United States.

> — *Boris O. Dittrich,*
> *First openly gay member of Dutch parliament*

Belgium (2003)

"Any enduring and loving relationship is appreciated in the same way in our modern society."

> — *Kristien Grauwels,*
> *Belgian legislator*

FROM WRONGS TO GAY RIGHTS

Spain (2005)

"Today, Spanish society is responding to a group of people who have been humiliated, whose rights have been ignored, their dignity offended, their identity denied and their freedom restricted."

— José Luis Rodíguez Zapatero,
Prime minister of Spain, 2004-11

Canada (2005)

"Rights are rights. None of us can or should pick and choose whose rights we will defend and whose rights we will ignore."

— Irwin Cotler,
Canadian member of parliament

South Africa (2006)

"When we attained our democracy, we sought to distinguish ourselves from an unjust painful past, by declaring that never again shall it be that any South African will be discriminated against on the basis of color, creed, culture and sex."

— Nosivive Mapisa-Nqakula,
S. Africa Home Affairs minister, 2004-09

Sweden (2009)

"It's important to welcome gay people to the church with all the same rights. Historically, you could say we have not been so accepting of gays and lesbians, but the church has become more open."

— Eva Brunne,
Vicar in the Church of Sweden

Norway (2009)

"The new law won't weaken marriage as an institution. Rather, it will strengthen it. Marriage won't be worth less because more can take part in it."

— Anniken Huitfeldt, Family Issues minister, on
introducing the bill in 2008

FROM WRONGS TO GAY RIGHTS

Portugal (2010)

"This law rights a wrong. ... It is a very important and symbolic step towards fully ensuring respect for values that are essential in any democratic, open and tolerant society: the values of freedom, equality and non-discrimination."

— José Sócrates,
Prime minister of Portugal, 2005-11

Argentina (2010)

"The vote came despite a lot of pressure [from the Catholic Church]. In the past, this would have influenced the votes of the senators. But not now."

— Fortunato Mallimaci,
Sociologist, University of Buenos Aire

Iceland (2010)

"The attitude in Iceland is fairly pragmatic. [Gay marriage] has not been a big issue in national politics. It has not been controversial."

— Gunnar Helgi Kristinsson,
Political scientist at the University of Iceland

Denmark (2012)

"This is equality between couples of the same gender and couples of different genders. A major step forward."

— Manu Sareen
Danish minister for ecclesiastical affairs

Parts of Mexico, Brazil and the United States

In Mexico, same-sex marriages are authorized in the Federal District (Mexico City, starting in 2009) and in the states of Quintana Roo (2011) and Oaxaca (2012).

In Brazil, same-sex marriages are allowed in the states of Alagoas, Bahia and São Paulo (all starting in 2012).

FROM WRONGS TO GAY RIGHTS

In the United States, same-sex marriage is legal in Massachusetts (starting in 2004), Connecticut (2008), Iowa (2009), Vermont (2009), New Hampshire (2010), Washington, D.C. (2010), New York (2011), Washington state (2012), Maine (2012) and Maryland (2013).

At the other extreme: Nigeria

In Nigeria, the Senate and House of Representatives have both voted in favor of a bill that would make same-sex marriage a criminal offense punishable by a 14-year prison sentence for the couple and a 10-year sentence for anyone assisting in the ceremony. A final vote on the bill had not been held by the time this book was published. If the bill is passed, it would then be sent to the president of Nigeria for him to sign or veto.

"We are protecting humanity and family values. In fact, we are protecting civilization in its entirety," says Nigerian Senator Ahmed Lawan, a supporter of the bill to outlaw same-sex marriage. "Should we allow for indiscriminate same-sex marriage, very soon the population of this world would diminish."

What traditional African homosexuality learned from the West

By ERIC O. LEMBEMBE

May 8, 2012 — Homosexuality has a long history in Africa, says anthropologist Patrick Awondo, contrary to the claims of politicians who consider it a recent Western import.

But Awondo acknowledged in an interview that two key elements in the debate over homosexuality in Africa did come from the West — first, colonial-era laws against homosexual activities and, more recently, the establishment of groups opposing discrimination against gays, lesbians and transgender people.

"Homosexuality has always existed, but some of the current forms of gay self-identification and gay activism originated elsewhere," he said. Awondo was in Cameroon last month to help lead a training session on HIV/AIDS.

Citing historical records of homosexual practices in Africa, Awondo mentioned evidence of same-sex sexual relationships in Cameroon, Zimbabwe, Burkina Faso and Benin.

FROM WRONGS TO GAY RIGHTS

It is helpful for Africans to know about ancient practices such as Mossi kings' sexual relations with their pages and marriages between women in Dahomey, he said.

"Knowing historical truths lets us avoid unhistorical lies," he said.

Patrick Awondo

Awondo has a doctorate in political sociology and medical anthropology from the School for Advanced Studies in the Social Sciences in Paris. A translation of his interview with Cameroonian journalist Eric O. Lembembe appears below.

How long have you worked with the African Network for Training on HIV / AIDS?

I have been associated as an expert anthropologist for this group since March 2011 beginning in Ouagadougou, Burkina Faso, working with Dr. Jean-Baptiste Guiard-Schmid and Dr. Steave Nemande. I coordinate two sessions.

One focuses on socio-anthropological questions about MSM (men who have sex with men), specifically the question of sexual identity and sexual behavior of this group, its history on this continent and people's perceptions of it. Basically, why is it so difficult for people in Africa (as elsewhere) to accept a homosexual group?

In the second session, I help trace various groups' involvement in the fight against AIDS in Africa. How did people rally around these challenges, and how did that affect the fight against AIDS for populations most at risk? We train health professionals to distinguish between sexual identity and sexual behavior — a distinction that is very important for public health.

More and more these days, debates about homosexuality in Africa include the assertion that the practice comes from elsewhere — it never existed here, so it should be rejected totally. Can we say that homosexuality in Africa is a "Westernization" of African customs?

FROM WRONGS TO GAY RIGHTS

Training session run by the African Network for Training on HIV / AIDS in Cameroon

Given the work of historians, anthropologists and some archaeologists, it is difficult to say that homosexuality is a Western influence, since it seems increasingly clear that there is a history of homosexual practices throughout the continent. That is well documented, but it is also clear that human societies everywhere have often put up strong resistance to "normalization" of homosexuality. All societies tend to look on homosexuality and homosexual practices as a threat to their survival or to their stability, even though the validity of that idea has never been verified.

From my point of view, what can be considered "Westernization" is not only the criminalization of homosexuality by post-colonial states — since, as we know, most of the laws introduced against homosexuality are modeled after those of colonial powers — but also the emergence of a social and political group that claims its homosexual identity as a political identity. By demanding rights based on sexual practices, they make homosexuality a political issue. This emergence of a homosexual identity is marked by a social lifestyle and identification with the "gay culture" that developed first in the United States in the late 1960's and then in Western Europe.

Yes, identification with this lifestyle to some extent may be "Westernization." But, let us be clear, this is a "Westernization" as one might say that democracy is "Western," since its present form emerged from a specific location is the West, or at least part of what we call the West. But the principle of the pursuit of liberty is universal.

Simply put, homosexuality has always existed, but some of the current forms of gay self-identification and gay activism originated elsewhere, then inspired similar developments in other countries, including countries in Africa.

Does the practice of homosexuality play a role in the histories of African customs? Please give examples, if possible.

As a social scientist, I will refer you to others' work in this field. First, the short, very fine work of Murray and Roscoe, published in 1998 under the title "Boy Wives and Female Husbands: Studies of African Homosexualities." It tells of the early work of anthropologists and explorers throughout the continent, sometimes even during their initial contact with Africans, who described what was said about homosexuality by the people who at that time were called the "natives."

Also worth mentioning is the work of historian Marc Epprecht, including his fine book "Hungoschani. A Story of a Dissident Sexuality in Southern Africa," which traces the history of homosexual practices in the area now known as Zimbabwe.

I used some of these works in my Ph.D. thesis and I devoted a chapter to homosexuality among the Beti of Cameroon, as seen in pre-colonial traditions such as the "mevungu" ritual of a secret society for women. Analysis of "indigenous" speech, first collected by ethnologists, sheds light on what homosexuality represented in those cultures, along with their discussions about it, which indicates that both homosexuality and debate about it have always existed.

How did African gays live before the era of globalization (or colonization)?

It is difficult to answer such a question because, as I have said, the category "homosexual" was not really recognized as it is today.

The situations for those people were very different depending on where they lived in the region, their class, their age, and other sociological characteristics.

Specifically, homosexual practices were not the same for a king, as among the Mossi of Burkina Faso today, and for a page in the king's service in the same region and in the same group.

Pages, including young men sometimes disguised as women, could play the role of a woman for the king in certain circumstances where it was forbidden to touch women.

When he had homosexual relations with his pages, it was more or less recognized and "institutionalized."

Melville Herkovits also described "marriages" between women in the ancient kingdom of Dahomey, now Benin.

In this case women — often wealthy older women — sometimes married women in the absence of men. These wives could have lovers, and their children were recognized as those of the "husband-wife."

There are all sorts of configurations on the continent. Historians' work must continue, not as propaganda, but because it is good to know our history — even the history that

Mossi mask

some people wish weren't true. Knowing historical truths lets us avoid unhistorical lies.

Why are same-sex relations so despised in Africa? Why are people afraid of homosexuals?

FROM WRONGS TO GAY RIGHTS

I'll mention some factors, including the recent history of colonization of the African continent, and the heterosexual norm of human societies. In addition, new meanings are placed on old practices — for example, what went on in ancient rituals is considered to be something that contributes to modern homosexual identity.

There are many causes, not one. One set of causes can be summarized as "postcolonial tensions." These tensions arise between the former colonial powers like France and African countries like Cameroon.

Some of these former colonial powers are now seen as "moral leaders" in defense of sexual minorities, even though that is debatable. Ongoing advocacy by these "moral leaders" in favor of universal decriminalization of homosexuality causes conservative reactions in many countries.

A concrete example?

For example, increased funding from the European Union to Cameroonian groups serving homosexuals provoked outrage from some in the news media and in politics in 2011.

This situation revives memories of colonialism, putting homosexuality at the heart of a postcolonial controversy. Africans are led to regard homosexuality as an expression of the decadence of the West.

The other current issue on the African continent is political leaders' reliance on criticizing society in order to build public support. The anthropologist Saskia Weiringa called this politicians' "moral sexual strategy." A variety of political actors use such strategies to make themselves known. This is true of all these groups of young people on the continent that publish texts "against homosexuality" even though, in reality, they are trying to make their voices heard on other issues, like corruption, nepotism, incompetent leadership, etc.

Besides all this, heterosexism is a universal fact, even though some analyses of "African homophobia" depict it as applying to Africa alone. The effects of the "norm of heterosexuality" and its macho partner — "phallocracy" — must also be considered seriously. All these facts and others may explain the negative perception of homosexuality on the continent.

The fatal flaw
in anti-AIDS strategies

By COLIN STEWART

When public health officials, doctors and researchers gathered in July 2012 for the International AIDS Conference, they proclaimed their support for a plan to "end AIDS in our lifetimes."

Unfortunately, their strategies have a fatal shortcoming. Summarized in the "Washington DC Declaration," the plan outlines nine strategies for fighting AIDS, but fails to mention the tragic consequences of 76-plus nations' laws against homosexuality, which effectively exclude LGBT people from receiving AIDS-related services.

Dr. Elly Katabira, president of the International AIDS Society and international chair of last summer's conference, introduced the declaration optimistically, stating, "In a scenario unthinkable just a few years ago, we now have the knowledge to begin to end AIDS in our lifetimes."

Several of the strategies in the declaration come close to the issue of anti-homosexuality laws, though none addresses it directly. But without repeal of those laws, the following strategies in the Washington DC Declaration cannot be implemented:

FROM WRONGS TO GAY RIGHTS

- "Ensure evidence-based HIV prevention, treatment and care in accord with the human rights of those at greatest risk and in greatest need. This includes men who have sex with men, transgender individuals, people who use drugs, vulnerable women, young people, pregnant women living with HIV, and sex workers, as well

Elly Katabira of Uganda, president of the International AIDS Society.

as other affected populations. No one can be excluded if we are to reach our goal." *But if LGBT people are defined as criminals, they WILL be excluded.*

- "End stigma, discrimination, legal sanctions and human rights abuses against people living with HIV and those at risk. Stigma and discrimination hamper all our efforts and prevent delivery of essential services." *But if LGBT people are defined as criminals, they WILL be stigmatized and discriminated against.*

- "Markedly increase HIV testing, counseling and linkages to prevention, care and support services. Every person has a right to know her/his HIV status and get the treatment, care and support they need." *But in countries where LGBT people are defined as criminals, they often are excluded from such services.*

- "Expand access to antiretroviral treatment to all in need. We cannot end AIDS until the promise of universal access is realized." *Again, where LGBT people are defined as criminals, they often are denied access to needed treatment.*

- "Mobilization and meaningful involvement of affected communities must be at the core of collective responses. The leadership of those directly affected is paramount to an effective HIV/AIDS response." *But where LGBT people are defined as criminals, they rarely will be allowed to become leaders of the fight against HIV/AIDS.*

FROM WRONGS TO GAY RIGHTS

Anti-homosexuality laws are part of the reason why estimated HIV infection rates are higher for men who have sex with men, or MSM, than for the general population in countries such as these:

- Benin: estimated adult HIV infection rate of 1.2 percent, according to UNAIDS, but 25.5 percent for MSM.
- Ghana: 1.8 percent overall, but 25 percent for MSM.
- Guyana: 1.2 percent overall, but 19.4 percent to 21.3 percent for MSM.
- Indonesia: 0.2 percent overall, but 5.2 percent for MSM.
- Jamaica: 1.7 percent overall, but 25 percent to 31.8 percent for MSM.
- Kenya: 6.3 percent overall, but 10.6 percent to 43 percent for MSM.
- Malaysia: 0.5 percent overall, but 3.9 percent to 7 percent for MSM,
- Nigeria: 3.6 percent overall, but 13.5 percent for MSM.
- Sudan: 1.1 percent overall, but 8.8 percent to 9.3 percent for MSM.
- Uganda: 6.5 percent overall, but 12.4 percent to 32.9 percent for MSM.
- Zambia: 13.5 percent overall, but 32.9 percent for MSM.

Laws against homosexuality are an obstacle to victory in the fight against AIDS. Strategies ignoring that fact are strategies for failure.

FROM WRONGS TO GAY RIGHTS

ISSUES OF FAITH

FROM WRONGS TO GAY RIGHTS

And the archbishop wondered: Dildos for the widows of Uganda?

Modern-day Uganda is a hotbed of anti-gay agitation, with the Church of Uganda often rejecting any suggestions that LGBT people deserve respect rather than punishment. It was not always thus, as the Rev. Canon Albert Ogle describes in this account of the early 1990s.

By THE REV. CANON ALBERT OGLE

Yona Okoth was the Anglican Archbishop of Uganda from 1984 to 1995. He described himself as " just a man from the jungle" and rose from obscurity to head the 10-million-member Church of Uganda, representing a third of his country's population.

I met him in 1991 when he asked for help to combat the spread of AIDS.

He had an "AIDS conversion experience" in 1988 after he dramatically spoke at the Lambeth Conference of worldwide Anglican bishops.

"We do not have AIDS in Africa," he had said, and all the African bishops agreed with him. He returned to Uganda to find his driver had killed himself, and the driver's children and grandchildren were infected with the deadly virus. He spent the rest of his ministry tirelessly working to prevent the spread of the disease.

I would arrange tours for him in the USA and the UK where we would raise funds and support for his AIDS work. Hundreds of thousands of dollars were raised by Yona through grants from USAID and congregations like mine in south Orange County, California.

Archbishop Yona Okoth

Other African bishops would also come over, including Bishop William Rukirande from Kabale, Uganda, to raise money for his AIDS orphans. (Many of the bishops were taking care of the children of dead relatives of local community children.) My congregation – gay and straight people alike — gave him thousands of dollars to educate and feed these destitute children, one of whom was David Bahati — William's now infamous ward.

Bahati would grow up to become the Member of Parliament who introduced the draconian "Kill The Gays" bill that is still pending before the Ugandan parliament. Little did we know, LGBTQ money would support someone who has become the poster child of the USA Christian Right's anti-gay agenda in Africa.

Bahati became a member of "The Family," a secretive and highly influential network of international "born-again" politicians and religious leaders who have tried to impose a theocratic view of the world upon many African countries in the past 20 years. Bahati represents the present-day Church of Uganda that was bribed and eventually bought by American-led fundamentalists seeing homosexuality as inherently evil and an imposition of Western decadence.

Bahati is absolutely convinced that the Western gay agenda is focused on recruiting hundreds of thousands of Ugandan schoolchildren. His name has become so well known that he has become an international celebrity of sorts.

FROM WRONGS TO GAY RIGHTS

What Bahati fails to communicate is the positive and philanthropic role that Western LGBTQ people played in his own upbringing. Where Bahati represents a church and state that has led the world in homophobic misinformation, Yona represents an African religious leader who did not have a homophobic bone in his body.

In the mid-1990s, Yona and I were in Atlanta for a series of events and speaking engagements and he was the guest of honor at an art gallery opening. The gallery was owned by an attractive lesbian couple and the evening was elegant and engaging.

Yona was enjoying all the attention poured on him by this largely lesbian community who wrote many checks for his AIDS work. At the end of the evening, we said goodnight and ran through the rainy streets to our car to return to our hotel. As I started the engine and turned on the windscreen wipers, the Archbishop asked me a very difficult question:

"Albert, what do lesbi-yans DO?"

Swish, swish, swish, swish went the sliding wiper blades as they cleared a way for me to see the road ahead and as I hunted for an appropriate response in this teachable moment.

The Archbishop knew I was gay and never had an issue with that, but with all these beautiful women around him all evening, he was obviously curious as to the sexual practices of women who made love without men.

"Well, Your Grace, there are many ways to make love …"

I searched for words.

"Yes, but what do Lesbi-yans DOOO??" he asked with even more episcopal authority.

Swish-swish, swish-swish, swish-swish. The wiper blades moved even faster.

"Well …. they use their tongues and fingers like heterosexual couples do!"

This was still clearly not enough information to quell his African heterosexual search for truth.

"And they sometimes use dildos," I stammered.

"What's a dildo?" my now engaged passenger asked.

I was glad the car was dark and he couldn't see my red face! This was what parents must go through when the kids want to know everything about the birds and the bees. But he was really interested and engaged, and so the conversation needed more truth. I couldn't just delay his questions for a later conversation with a lesbian, so we continued:

"It is an artificial penis, Your Grace."

Swish-swish, swish-swish.

Silence. Then "Mmmmmmmmmmm" — the deep sound that many Africans make, which usually means "how very interesting."

"They are usually made of rubber or plastic."

I thought the African continent might be familiar with wooden versions of a dildo and I had certainly seen phallic African art and fetish objects before, so was he completely oblivious to sex toys, I wondered?

There was a long silence with more swish-swishing through the rainy Atlanta night. I couldn't wait to arrive at our hotel and escape the African sexual inquisition.

Yona had admitted on many occasions how difficult it was for Ugandan heterosexuals to discuss intimate sexual issues when it came to AIDS prevention. The British missionaries to Uganda had certainly ensured their "position" would remain the dominant one – guilt, shame and all. But we had a great open relationship and I loved his courage and leadership.

He wanted to know something new and these strong Southern women had intrigued him. He was also not afraid to wave a condom or two in his Kampala cathedral to make his point clear that ABC (Abstinence, Be Careful and Condom use) were tools to help people survive AIDS.

Millions of condoms were distributed under USAID's auspices to his churches and millions of lives were saved by his courage.

Then he had a eureka moment.

"We should have dildos for the widows of Uganda!" he exclaimed.

More swishing.

I immediately imagined a new campaign we could wage among gay and lesbian bars throughout the country, where barrels could be placed to collect dildos "for the widows of Uganda." God knows, there were millions of them.

Archbishop Yona had figured out a way Ugandan women, who may have been infected with AIDS by their late husbands, could continue to find some pleasure in life. It was completely rational and without any guile or homophobia. It was also a deep humane and compassionate response. He was thinking of ways he could help his people live with this terrifying disease.

It was probably one of the most beautiful and honest conversations I have ever had with a friend and ally, where our different sexualities were honored and extremely humorous! Here was an African in whom there was not only no guile, but no homophobia.

Yona will always represent the best of African spirituality and sexuality. It is amazing to think where the Church of Uganda stands today and where it was under Yona's leadership

In the wake of billions of dollars of Bush Administration "faith based" initiatives in Africa, the ABC's of HIV prevention would be replaced by "abstinence only," family planning funding would be prohibited and anti-LGBT evangelists would be free to lie and bribe their way to the Bahati era we now witness. The fruit of the Christian Right in Africa is rotting and the stench of political and religious corruption is disguised by a so called "pro-family" agenda.

We can trace this infusion of USA Christian fundamentalist homophobia back to the late 1990s when Yona retired and was replaced by Archbishop Livingstone Mpalanyi Nkoyoyo. The Church of Uganda was always evangelical and conservative, but never homophobic as it is today.

Nkoyoyo attended the 1998 Lambeth Conference of Anglican bishops and opened the floodgates for American fundamentalism to import its homophobic agenda on millions of Africans. (Half of the 76 countries where it is still illegal to be LGBTQ are in Sub-Saharan Africa.) This agenda continued under Archbishop Henry Orombi, who supported the Bahati bill [through his retirement in late 2012].

Multiply Uganda by 75 times and you begin to see the power of rigid religious fundamentalism in mainstream churches like the Anglican and Roman Catholic Church. The wave of neo-colonial evangelism in Africa also meant more progressive churches withdrew from Africa or were disinvited by the new wave of Archbishops. ...

Yona will always be my hero. His wonderful humor was an antidote to the recent homophobia that has been imposed upon his beloved church and his country. He represented the best of what Africa can be and my hope is that we get through today's dark and frightening tunnel as soon as possible and return to a shared focus on the eradication of poverty, ignorance and disease.

Finding kindred spirits among straight allies in the faith community

Twenty-six LGBT activists traveled to the International AIDS Conference in Washington, D.C., in mid-2012, seeking to change a world where homosexuality is illegal in 76-plus countries. In this article, the Rev. Canon Albert Ogle, founder of St. Paul's Foundation for International Reconciliation, describes how straight allies supported them, and what the supporters learned in the process.

By THE REV. CANON ALBERT OGLE

When I spoke at Good Shepherd parish in Silver Spring, Md., about the plight of LGBT people internationally, it was April 14, 2012, the anniversary of the sinking of the Titanic. Here was an average suburban Washington, D.C. congregation who had no connection with the 76 countries where it is illegal to be LGBT.

The question posed to the congregation was this: If we can find people to travel to Washington to represent those countries and their issues, would you host them to stay in your homes during the International AIDS Conference? If they also address the congregation and tell you

FROM WRONGS TO GAY RIGHTS

The Rev. Canon Albert Ogle

what it is like for them living under this kind of oppression, would you also support their work when they would return home?

St. Paul's Foundation and our Washington-based volunteers worked with 50 congregations during the spring and summer, and 12 agreed to host one of our delegates.

This was completely uncharted territory for all of us. It was also difficult work.

The subject of HIV and LGBT in most Washington congregations is not something good Christian people want to talk about. A progressive mosque initially wanted to sponsor a delegate but during the last week pulled out.

In a city that has HIV infection rates as high as some African countries, the International AIDS Conference brought some attention to an issue most congregations did not want to deal with, so these 12 congregational opportunities we had were priceless.

We called the local volunteer hosts "shepherds" because they would represent a pastoral and supportive role to our international guests. Most of our visitors had never been to the USA before, so this would be their first encounter with ordinary American domestic life and a worshipping congregation who did not endorse hellfire and damnation for LGBT people.

I returned to D.C. six weeks after the conference to see what impact the visitors and their stories had on the shepherds and their congregations.

I discovered that the impact was profound. One retired married couple had provided a base for Macdonald Sembereka, an Anglican priest living in Malawi. He is HIV-positive and part of an international network of 7,000 HIV-positive religious leaders called INERELA.

FROM WRONGS TO GAY RIGHTS

As a straight advocate for LGBT inclusion, Macdonald experienced so much stigma from his faith community that he now works to alleviate it for everyone. When he began to speak out in favor of decriminalization of LGBT people in Malawi, the mob turned on him. As legislators added lesbianism to the anti-gay penal code, someone firebombed Macdonald's home while his wife and children lay sleeping. This did not deter him from working to reduce discrimination against LGBT people. He focused largely on homophobia in churches and began to organize a conference for religious leaders and politicians to discuss this issue.

We assigned Macdonald to Good Shepherd in the hope there would be good chemistry between him and his hosts. Sure enough, the report from the two retired teachers who welcomed him into their home was extremely encouraging.

Macdonald not only stayed with his new friends during the AIDS Conference, but also later when he visited D.C. to take part in a meeting of the Presidential AIDS Program (PEPFAR).

That time, while they were sitting at the dinner table, Macdonald's cell phone rang. He excused himself and began talking energetically, using the word "Excellency" a couple of times. As Malawi's new presidential adviser on Non Government Organizations (NGO), Macdonald was speaking with Joyce Banda, the president of Malawi. She was in New York trying to raise support to feed her 1.3 million starving people and was now on her way to Washington to build more support for her case.

Macdonald passed the phone to his host to say hello. Mary was eating her ice cream and didn't have time to figure out that she was speaking to a head of state. She remembered to call her "Your Excellency" and they had a conversation about Banda's Presbyterian past and the mission she was on in the USA. Mary told the president how Macdonald had changed their awareness about many international issues and how impressed they were that she was one of the few African heads of state willing to look seriously at repealing the anti-gay laws on her country's books.

Mary's congregation not only raised almost $3,000 to support the Spirit of 76 program to bring 26 international visitors to D.C., but also an additional $1,000 to support an orphanage Macdonald was helping. A little money for uniforms and school fees went a long way. The couple laughed and recounted how excited Macdonald was to shop at our bargain department stores for shoes and clothes for his orphans. He was particularly proud of one orphan who had made it to medical school.

The Silver Springs congregation is now supporting his work and Macdonald is welcome any time in Mary and Paul's home. Their tangible support of this one man is helping to change a country. Simply by opening their hearts and home, they allowed Macdonald find kindred spirits and the bread of angels to sustain him on a difficult journey towards equality.

'I had nowhere to live but in my car'

In mid-2012, after the International AIDS Conference ended in Washington, D.C., the 26 activists brought there by the Spirit of 76 Worldwide project returned to their home countries, where some of them faced immediate retaliation.

By THE REV. CANON ALBERT OGLE

Only 10 days after the Spirit of 76 initiative was celebrated in Washington, D.C., one of our bright and talented African activists was deliberately targeted by his government for retaliation.

His crime: He attended the International AIDS Conference and was sponsored by St. Paul's Foundation.

He was suspended from his job, deprived of his salary, and lost his home and support base within a week of his return home. Both he and his partner are now homeless and are living in fear of being arrested, subjected to mob violence or being killed.

Only two weeks before, Samuel (not his real name) sat in a conference room at the World Bank in Washington, D.C., and talked about why the bank needs to do more for LGBT people globally. If their mission is to end global poverty, then they have to seriously look at the effects and impact of systemic homophobia upon the lives of millions of invisible LGBT people who are often only a day or two away from living on the streets, deprived of rights and employment.

Well-educated and successful professionals can become street people without the protection of government just for being perceived to be LGBT criminals. The 26 international visitors gave examples of how this happens in education, healthcare and business — all areas where the World Bank is actively working with governments in most of the 76 countries where it is still illegal to be LGBT.

No one had significantly made this connection before to such a powerful institution, we were later told. The four World Bank executives took notes and shared some of the bank's internal processes and wanted this group to help them achieve their mission.

What was an academic description for Samuel two weeks ago now became his family's personal nightmare as his government began the process of dehumanization -- depriving people of constitutional rights and their ability to earn a living and be contributing members of society.

For the past 10 years, Samuel worked hard for a government agency and was climbing the ladder of his professional field. His presence at the International AIDS Conference, and his concern for access to health and rights for LGBT people globally, cost him and his partner the thin plank they were standing upon dividing normalcy from chaos. A government agency yanked it away and they both plunged into the abyss of "non persons."

This is precisely why 26 people came to Washington in the first place – to make sure governments or churches are not allowed to treat LGBT as non-citizens or non-persons who are not protected under civil or religious law, even the law of loving one's neighbor.

Samuel is a practicing Roman Catholic. When the Vatican makes a statement like "Homosexuality is not an identity, merely a set of intrinsically disordered behaviors," the church participates in the wanton destruction of otherwise creative and loving lives and relationships such as Samuel's. Many of the religious leaders I know who advocate this position do not think about its consequences. They may be wonderful pastors, caring for widows and orphans, the homeless and the oppressed, but when it comes to LGBT people, their own fear allows their shadow side to create the damaging situations that they and their organizations are trying to heal.

If religious leaders could begin to make that connection, we might find ourselves on a different trajectory. Otherwise, Rick Warren or the local Cardinal will merely walk by on the other side and allow a form of institutional bullying to take its course. The underlying and unspoken goal is to make life as difficult as possible for LGBT people in the hope they just stop talking about it, never mind "doing it."

Samuel's sin, in their eyes, is not just that he is homosexual but also that he has the audacity to talk about it and to see it as a part of his identity. Further, he is challenging the government's policy of depriving LGBT criminals of their constitutional rights and health services.

Even though Samuel is a devout Catholic, he would be hard-pressed to find any bishop or priest to come out publicly and say that what the government is doing to him is morally wrong.

This was one of my concerns from the International AIDS Conference — Rick Warren, the Vatican and most liberal churches were patting each other on the back so much that they did not see the wounded ones like Samuel. After all, the church is caring for so many widows, orphans and the sick that no one is particularly concerned about a few queers who are going to hell anyway.

The institutional damage of religious homophobia in half the world remains unfettered, despite our efforts at the conference. It was significant to notice that 40 percent of our 26 international activists (gay and straight) were practicing Catholics. The church persecutes its own baptized. The clergy are walking on the other side of the street while the bound and beaten LGBT community picks up fragmented lives.

Samuel and his partner had to literally pick up the pieces of their lives thrown into the street. I cannot imagine what it is like to be hounded in this way while some of the institutions we trust, and are even inspired by, walk by on the other side. It is ironic that Jesus deliberately chose clergy as the embodiment of self-absorbed and self-protected individuals who crossed the road to avoid dealing with the beaten man in the parable of the Good Samaritan. It is from the margins and in surprising places that we will find help and rescue, not from professional do-gooders.

Yet these young people who made up the Spirit of 76 still believe in the institutions that are making their lives hell. They are reformers rather than anarchists. They believe in the power of their stories and in their personal courage to win hearts and minds. They are an inspiration to all of us who usually take so much of our own freedom and ability to thrive professionally for granted.

Only three weeks ago I saw Samuel smiling and hugging some of his new-found friends in Washington in a bar where he was just like any other twentysomething. How quickly things can change. But his determination to share with his community back home what we all take for granted in the USA must get our respect and attention -- even the most jaded and complacent among us.

St. Paul's Foundation wired him some emergency money so they could rent a place to live and buy food, have access to a phone and computer, and reach out to Samuel's new-found Spirit of 76 network. It was that simple and it made such a difference to their sense of personal security.

Samuel wants to regroup, hire an attorney and continue to work for the dignity and rights of all. He wants to get his job back or do something that will be even more significant for the cause he feels so passionate about. I wonder what you or I might have done if we faced a similar ordeal?

Bishop Christopher Senyonjo

Bishop Christopher: Theological leper steps out in faith

By THE REV. CANON ALBERT OGLE

For more than a decade, Bishop Christopher Senyonjo has been under pressure from the Anglican Church of Uganda because he has refused to condemn LGBT people. In the 12 years since his retirement, the church has tried everything to get him to recant. They removed his ability to function as a bishop so he was unable to make a living or have a retirement plan. They would not allow him to perform marriages or baptize his grandchildren. The ultimate threat to bury him in unconsecrated ground still hangs over his head and brings tears to his sparkling eyes.

His family has also been through a decade-long nightmare. Press reports about him defamed his reputation as a senior religious leader.

When the Church of Uganda supported the "Kill the Gays" bill two years ago, Bishop Christopher was chosen by the coalition opposing it to present a million signatures to the Speaker of the Ugandan parliament. The Huffington Post selected him as one of the world's Top 10 most influential religious leaders

What is the secret to this man's courage in the face of so many odds?

When I met the bishop two and a half years ago, he was in a deep economic and spiritual hole. The bishop's family was trying to convince him to give up his public support of LGBT people. His 10-year financial support from Integrity USA had dried up. He had to sell some of his family land to make ends meet. His faith kept him going and a close pastoral relationship to LGBT people convinced him that he should "hang in there" and continue to do the right thing. Many of his clergy and bishop friends have deserted him. He was considered a theological leper. Several clergy who continued to support him also suffered persecution from the Archbishop. Yet against all odds today the bishop runs a thriving St. Paul's Centre for Reconciliation and Equality with nine full-time employees.

He is not just a success story — his story is a miracle. Sometimes we all have to step forward in faith, often without any resources, but knowing that one day, one's work and values will be honored and blessed. Faith is not about certainty. There is something inside us that challenges us to step out and believe there will be ground below our step, or we will find a way to fly.

He literally had nothing two years ago and today he is known throughout the world as the Desmond Tutu of Uganda. He was selected by the San Francisco Pride Parade to be one of its grand marshals. He rode through the streets of San Francisco with a million people celebrating LGBT Pride. His story is important at this crucial moment in LGBT history because it is about thriving.

What is it that has kept this 80-year-old going? Christopher's values are based on the values of Jesus and St. Paul. All three were never populists. They all have a vision of full inclusion in a newly energized humanity.

Christopher's story is about making the right decisions, which may fly in the face of your family and church, and thriving against all odds.

Homophobia:
'I too am infected'

By THE REV. CANON ALBERT OGLE

In 1987, I became the first openly gay priest at All Saints Church in Pasadena, Calif., which has become the largest inclusive Episcopal congregation west of the Mississippi. Five year earlier, I had arrived in Los Angeles and met with the rector, George Regas. I asked him to support my work with LGBT runaway and throwaway youth.

Although a courageous defender of justice, George was not ready to take on gay issues. It was 1982 and he gave me a check for $300 and sent me on my way. I returned to his office in 1987, suggesting he hire me to begin the AIDS Service Center ministry. Again, George was reluctant to move into this new and controversial territory and pondered my request for three months. Then he hired me to develop a new ministry.

For the next three years, I would discover that institutional homophobia was alive and well at All Saints.

It was painful to sit with other colleagues in a staff meeting where senior clergy denounced any participation by All Saints parishioners in the Los Angeles Pride celebrations. It was uncomfortable to hear how a gay couple had been counseled by another priest "to just go and take a cold shower." When the church notice board was repainted and placed outside with all the clergy names on it except mine, I had to challenge this decision. The reason given to me was that I was not "real parish clergy" but only the director of the AIDS Service Center.

Homophobia makes us invisible, or "less than," and I challenged the decision. If I was important enough to serve at the altar, my name should be on the church notice board with everyone else!

I found support and comfort in friendship with an experienced African-American priest on staff, Lo Wooden. He had witnessed a lynching as a young man and worked in the civil rights movement with Dr. Martin Luther King Jr. He now found himself, in his own words, as a pastor in the "dining room" of affluent white America.

We were both very much "outsiders" from the typical All Saints membership and Wooden gave me enormous support during those early difficult years.

For example, when I asked George if he would bless the relationship of my partner and me, he refused. It wasn't personal -- he told many LGBT couples the same thing. I watched him wrestling with his own demons on this issue.

George was a consummate politician as well as a pastor. He had a very large heart but he was not going to move out into uncharted territory without some allies. I watched him carefully gain support from other "cardinal rectors" in places like New York before he personally moved forward on "the gay issue."

I remember attending an all day event he had planned at St. Bartholomew's in New York. He invited my partner and me and a lesbian couple with two children to come to New York. The All Saints mantra at this time was: "We want to be a family parish, so God sent a lesbian couple with two kids!" They were amazing.

The four of us became the voices of faithful LGBT people to these powerful churchmen. We shared our faith stories and how the homophobia of the church had severely impacted us. Telling our stories to these strangers was "a turning point," as George said in a personal note of thanks to us. He sensed he was on a journey and he began to listen to us and to his own heart.

FROM WRONGS TO GAY RIGHTS

Several months later, I had a frank discussion with George about homophobia. I will never forget it. I saw all the tension in him leave his face and body when I admitted to him I was homophobic too. He looked puzzled because he had been tortured with the belief that homophobia was an exclusively heterosexual problem.

The Rev. Dr. George Regas

"I am homophobic too, George!" I blurted out, "because I live in the same world you do that has taught me all my life that my love is not good. This message is ingrained in me as much as it is in you. I have to deal with it more urgently than you because it is about me!"

George's jaw dropped and I could see a light bulb illuminate inside his tortured head. He desperately wanted to do the right thing but he struggled with years of heterosexual privilege. He confessed he had a hard time thinking about two guys kissing in front of him just after he married them.

It wasn't the relationship that gave him problems, it was the symbolism — a bit of straight "yuk" factor. He now had permission from a gay priest to be homophobic and not pretend he wasn't. He was on the same journey and continuum that I was on and every other person on the planet. It was a journey of self-discovery and a way the institutional church could hold onto its cherished values and beliefs but include us, not exclude.

I worked at All Saints from 1987 to 1991 and it was extremely challenging, not only because of the AIDS work but also because of the work we all had to do on our collective homophobia. I made deep and lasting relationships with clergy and colleagues, parishioners and community members who are still very much in my life. It was not easy but it was real.

It was liberating to see how straight and gay folk could heal each other in the process and the AIDS Service Center was our love child. It was the first AIDS center in California that was purposefully designed as a gay/straight alliance, unlike many of the LGBT models that had emerged from the crisis. I had worked in many LGBT organizations previous to working in this largely heterosexual world. The self-destruction within the LGBT community was as present then as it is with us today. I have worked in many LGBT and AIDS organizations and the internalized homophobia and "turning the guns in on one another" is the underbelly of systemic sabotage that is a direct consequence of seeing homophobia only in the "other" and not in ourselves.

Twenty-five years later, All Saints has largely forgotten its difficult journey towards wholeness. By 1992, George took the courageous step to bless the first gay union, of Phil and Mark, and they asked me to lead the prayers that historic day.

The parish did not change overnight either. George carefully and deliberately spent a year discussing the issues with the congregation, who remained bitterly divided. As a good rector, he could read the congregation. I began to understand his caution in hiring me. The underlying fear of the institution was articulated in the mantra - "We do not want to become a gay church." This is a normal fear of any congregation that begins its journey to wholeness through repentance of its corporate homophobia.

Ironically, the opposition became a strange instrument of God's justice, changing the congregation from bystanders into allies. It was only when the Religious Right began picketing Sunday services, subjecting parishioners and even their young children to verbal abuse and sexual innuendo as they prepared for Sunday worship, that the majority of parishioners were finally converted

The same people who were afraid we would become a gay church experienced the same insults and bullying that LGBT people have struggled with all our lives. They got it.

FROM WRONGS TO GAY RIGHTS

The institution moved from being part of the bullying that is characteristic of most Christians to becoming a neutral bystander and finally, thanks to the behavior of the Religious Right, to being a place of welcome and full inclusion. As we see this process playing out on a national and international scale, the bullying of the Religious Right will help change hearts and minds as the last stage in our journey to wholeness.

Research shows that if people intervene within 10 seconds to a bullying incident on a playground, the bullying ends immediately. The bully is confronted and the bystanders are converted into allies. The focus shifts: The majority stops merely observing the bully and the victim. It becomes a participant, which ends the violence and breaks the cycle.

This is the secret to healing homophobia. It never quite leaves us fully, rooted as it is in a larger system of gender roles and sexism, but we can transform it. There is great work being done right now to help the church realize its collusion and participation in the destruction of millions of beautiful lives by either continuing to bully LGBT people (as we see in places like Uganda and 75 other countries where it is illegal to be LGBT) or remaining passive bystanders who allow the bullying to take place.

Meanwhile, in the churches, closeted clergy and lay leaders continue to be significant forces for status quo at best and often for negative reinforcement of stereotypes that impede the journey toward wholeness. The "ex-gay" movement is ironically full of people just like us. They are not monsters or evil people. Their internalized homophobia is so strong they are prepared to lie and deceive millions of people rather than face their own truth. They are distracted from this important self-reflection by building a pseudo-scientific global platform upon which nations create laws to send us to prison or execute us. The damage done by these underground cell groups, often meeting in evangelical churches like Saddleback and Skyline, needs to be exposed.

The Vatican remains a sanctuary for closeted clergy who never blinked an eyelid when the Episcopal Church began ordaining women but had a hissy fit when Gene Robinson was consecrated bishop, because Gene came out. For our closeted gay brothers, they would rather see a witch hunt unfold within the church, join forces with Mormons and fundamentalist Christians to fight LGBT people and spend millions of dollars doing so, than face their own sexuality.

We can blame President Ronald Reagan for not addressing AIDS for years until his friend Rock Hudson died, but what about his closeted speech writers who made sure the President never mentioned that dreaded "A" word? Such sins of omission are as harmful as everyday sins. The consequences of the deep unconscious decisions to demean, ignore or punish gender non-conformists need to be clearly brought to the light. Closeted clergy also believe they are helping us by remaining close to the centers of power. History will judge them as much as it judges Reagan's speech writers.

I am tired of listening to the excuses of large and well-funded LGBT organizations for not doing more for LGBT people globally, just because we are fighting for marriage equality in several U.S. states at the same time. What is stopping

The Rt. Rev. Gene Robinson

the Human Rights Campaign from doing much, much more for the millions of LGBT people who will die in the next decade because their governments deny them access to HIV prevention information or health care? Sadly, it is because the vast majority of the HRC board and donors do not see international LGBT work as having much support in the American LGBT community.

With a new HRC president, I pray we may see a conversion process happening in our own hearts that we usually only look for in "the other side." If enough people speak up among those of us who donate time and money to the good work HRC is doing, there is no reason why it cannot focus on both domestic and international issues.

The Religious Right has been doing this for years. We cannot expect churches to change and see their responsibility and their participation in human suffering if we are not willing to undergo a little self-reflection and change of heart of our own.

As the prayer says, "Racism still holds us in bondage. Sexism weighs us down. Heterosexism infects us." I would add "Homophobia is killing us." So, dear God, "Reform and call us with your truth."

Hateful comments, semi-loving responses

A selection of readers' comments on the Erasing 76 Crimes blog and responses from the blog's editor, Colin Stewart:

Everyone has a choice

Comment from Laventure Alix: I think that everyone has a choice about what life-style he or she wants to live, and we as human being must not judge or kill a gay person, just because he or she chooses to live the alternative life-style.

I am a Child of God. I do not support homosexuality or any organization that promotes it.

Homosexuality is a decision that a person makes, not a birth mark. But I feel that everybody has the right to be whatever they want to: gay or straight.

God has given human beings living on this earth free-will, whether they follow his standards or follow the life-styles of the majority that deliberately disobey JEHOVAH GOD.

Sexual preference is part of God's creation

Response: Thanks for the comment, but you underestimate the extent to which sexual preference is part of God's creation rather than a personal choice. Do you really believe that you CHOOSE (each day?) whether you'll be heterosexual or homosexual and then, I assume in your case, choose to be attracted to the opposite sex? Thanks for visiting the blog. Do come back.

Fags doom nations

Comment from Igor: Fags doom nations. Jude 1:7. God hates fags and fag enablers. Leviticus 18:22. Romans 1:25-27,32.

You misunderstand the words you cite

Response: Hi, Igor — I'll pass over your abusive language in order to get to a few points where I hope I can communicate with you seriously about how I think you're misunderstanding the words you're citing.

Jude 1:7 is about the punishment for those who, like Sodom and Gomorrah, give themselves over to "sexual immorality and perversion." You believe that's homosexuality, but the account in Genesis 19 makes clear that their sins are inhospitality and attempted rape. Rape surely counts as "sexual immorality and perversion."

It's true that Leviticus 18:22 is about male-male sex, which is described as "detestable," or "an abomination" — one of many acts that are described that way in the Old Testament. Equally bad, in terms of the Israelites' relationship with God, are eating with Egyptians, eating shellfish and accepting interest on a loan.

Unless you are an Ultra-Orthodox Jew, those restrictions aren't meant for you. They're specific rules that applied to the specific people thousands of years ago when they were in the midst of establishing their special relationship with Yahweh. Even if you take those rules to heart today, it's inconsistent to scorn gay men for their love, but not scorn all bankers for charging interest. It's hypocritical and hateful to scorn gay men for their love if you ever eat clam chowder.

I hope you'll devote some thought and prayer not only to that issue, but even more so to the Letter to the Romans, which contains a direct warning to people who show "no love, no mercy." (Romans 1:31) I must admit that your comments strike me as full of anger, without any love or mercy.

In the verses about immorality that you cite, St. Paul is leading up to an observation in Romans 2:1 about people "who pass judgment on someone else, for at whatever point you judge another, you are condemning yourself." Ouch! I read that as meaning that those who say, "God hates fags and fag enablers," are condemned by their own words.

I pray for your sake that, like St. Paul, you will turn your focus onto yourself and will see your way to living and writing with a heart that's without anger, full of love and mercy.

Religion is poison

Comment from Chowski: What else would you expect from ignorant bigots with religion-poisoned minds? "God" makes even the most reasonable person into a murderer.

Believers and non-believers get swept away

Response: *Hi, Chowski – Believers and non-believers alike sometimes get swept up into murderous attacks on those they disagree with. But I'll grant you that atheists and agnostics don't kill believers as often as vice versa. Cheers.*

Leave other nations alone

Comment from Sammy: In the cases where gays might face execution or extreme civil rights violations, yeah, but otherwise it's not our place to tell other nations what laws they should pass.

As an American, I've had enough of this world police BS. And quite frankly, with the actions of gay activists in this country I don't think I'd ever willingly jump on any bandwagon they provided since they're THE most irritating and hateful pieces of crap I've ever had the misfortune of encountering.

The ones who claim they're discriminated against the most are almost always 10 times as guilty as those they accuse for their own brands of hatred and intolerance.

We agree on one thing

Response: *Hi, Sammy -- It seems we agree on "the cases where gays might face execution or extreme civil rights violations," and that's the main focus of this blog. We differ on much of the rest. Thanks for visiting.*

Gays' identity crisis

Comment from Jack: Lets see…. For those who believe, God created man and woman to be together. For those who don't believe and believe in nature, male animals mate with female animals. OK, for those who believe in neither, they believe in the human intelligence, so you get female attempting to bond with female and male with male. Hmmmm. There seems to be an identity crisis amongst these so-called intelligent humans.

"Shake the dust off your sandals and never return. They are stiff-necked people"

Love your neighbor

Response: *Thanks for visiting, Jack. As I recall, one of the two great commandments is to love your neighbor as yourself. I'd say that should rule out throwing your neighbor into jail if he loves someone who doesn't conform to your understanding of who God wants him to love.*

Genes don't trump morality

Comment from Garot: If sexual preference (sexual desire in other words) is genetic, then aren't all pedophiles, necrophiliacs and zoophiliacs (people who have sex with animals) all normal? I mean you can't control your genes, right? So let us not try to control our desires or educate our children, let's just pretend it's all genetic – this way we don't have to feel responsible for our actions and degraded nature.

Get to know some decent, honest gay folks

Response: *Hi, Garot – Just in terms of logical argument, that's one of the better points that an anti-homosexuality debater can make.*

But there is a persuasive counter-argument, because you're equating categories that have crucial differences — particularly because there can be no equal consensual relationship for the sexual preferences that you list, except between consenting same-sex adults.

In real life, once you get to know decent, honest, caring people who are attracted to others of the same sex, you will find that your logical argument rings hollow.

No law will change reality or God's beliefs

Comment from "randomcitizen": You people do realize that no law you change will affect reality? You still won't be able to put a bolt into bolt, you still won't be able to have children, you won't be able to change God's beliefs no matter how much you complain, and you will never be accepted.

Sooner or later you're going to have to face that fact and stop referring to every group that decides to stand up for its morals a "hate group"

Seems to me the only hate group I've seen is a majority (but not all) of gays/lesbians. You spout acceptance but instantly jump on anyone or any group that doesn't see things your way. Might want to look up the definition of "equality."

Would-be killers qualify as hateful

Response: *Those who not only disagree with LGBT people, but also kill them because of their sexual identity, surely qualify as "hate groups."*

We will act if Uganda doesn't

Comment from "No Homo": If they don't pass the bill, we the nationals will take action. Mark my word.

You sadden me

Response: *Dear "No Homo" — By the phrase "take action," I guess you are implying that you and other non-homosexual Ugandans will act aggressively against people whose love you don't approve of. That saddens me. Why not just live and let live? (I don't believe the myth that gays seek to spread their lifestyle to children. Some people are born heterosexual; some are born homosexual. All are children of God.)*

Stop using Christian tax dollars for AIDS research

Comment from James: I just love how the homosexuals try and twist the BIBLE around to read what they want it to. It is because of such fools that prayer is no longer in schools. Everything that was moral is now just a memory to such stupidity. It does not break my heart 1 bit to see it illegal in these countries and totally believe it should be illegal in the USA.

I don't think it should be the responsibility of legal, moral Christians to pay for research into a disease that has been brought to us by homosexuals and dopers. If the government would stop using our tax dollars for education and research into the AIDS virus, just maybe the homosexuals and druggies would disappear as well — rather them then our Christian tax dollars.

That's so mean. And un-Christian

Response: *Hi, James — Do I have this right? As a Christian, you propose ending research into how to cure AIDS and you hope that people who contract the disease will die? Wow. That's so mean. And un-Christian.*

Still, I'll send some prayers your way.

PERSONAL STORIES

FROM WRONGS TO GAY RIGHTS

A night in hell, Zimbabwe style

Late on August 2012, Zimbabwe police raided the headquarters of the activist group Gays and Lesbians of Zimbabwe, seizing office equipment and arresting dozens of GALZ members. After police refused to return the property, the group decided to close the office. GALZ member Miles Tanhira describes here how that night's events affected her.

By MILES TANHIRA

I've always wondered what hell feels like. Now I know.

August 11 will always remain etched in my memories as a great day gone bad. What started off as a historic moment with the launch of our first-ever documentation of LGBT violations recorded in 2011 ended in tears and pain.

The drama began when we heard the guard alerting us that there were five policemen by the gate demanding to gain entry into the premises. Following procedure, the guard had asked for a search warrant and the police were getting agitated.

The police superior, who was seething with anger, was shouting at the guards, demanding that the gate be opened. He had parked his big white truck blocking the gate such that no one could get into the premises or come out.

FROM WRONGS TO GAY RIGHTS

GALZ compound in Harare, Zimbabwe

All this was happening while we were stuck inside. Fear of the unknown had gripped some who had already started jumping the huge security wall oblivious of the electric razor wire. Others who couldn't be bothered continued dancing to the music.

A few jumped and escaped safely. Others sustained injuries as they jostled to flee. A few unfortunate ones were caught by alert police officers who were manning the area after they discovered people were escaping.

In an hour's time, a human rights lawyer came into the premises and spoke with me. He said he was going to communicate with the police outside the gate but he never made it back inside.

How the riot squad, wearing helmets and armed with crowd-control button sticks, got into the premises still remains a point of confusion for me. All I remember is hearing orders for the DJ to stop the music and for everyone to sit or lie down where they were standing. The riot squad was violent, rowdy and screaming obscenities.

By then they had already started beating people up. They ordered us to move from the pool table area where most of us were gathered.

"Hold each other's belt, and move in a single file. If you use one hand to hold the next person's belt, you will get a thorough beating," they shouted.

When we got to the GALZ reception area, they made all of us sit by the driveway.

Button stick in action

"Switch off your cellphones. From now on there is no network, no talking, no smiling, no questioning, no movement or you will die," officers screamed.

An officer ordered one unfortunate guy sitting next to me to remove his colorful wrist band. While he was still doing that, he was summoned to the front, where three officers slapped him. Just as he sat down again, they discovered that his phone was still on. He was ordered to the front again.

They hit him hard with button sticks. Police shouted obscenities, and told him he was going to suffer once we got to their base. We were made to count ourselves by shouting numbers. Any mistake or stuttering warranted a beating.

After about ten minutes, we were told to stand up and repeat the belt-holding exercise. This time two officers made what they called a fence. If you failed to pass though you would be slapped. Once you got close to that fence they would lower it, making it impossible to pass through. Officers slapped and kicked us as we passed by. We got a thorough beating from different police officers.

IN THE TRUCK

GALZ members, including our guards, were force-marched into trucks parked outside. As we got into the back of the trucks we were slapped, beaten with the sticks and kicked. In the truck we were arbitrarily beaten and shouted at, using profanities.

The silence among us was deafening. If you dropped a needle you could have heard it fall. You could smell the fear in the truck. We didn't know where they were taking us. No one dared ask or say anything except for one colleague who said she had lost a phone and pleaded to get off the truck to look for it. Although some friends had seen a female officer picking it up, they couldn't tell her then for fear of being targeted for beatings.

While in the truck we got our feet stumped on and kicked for sitting comfortably and wasting space. The button sticks were used to hit our heads as we were ordered to make space for others to fit, like sardines. About 25 of us were packed in one small pickup truck. When our colleague returned without her phone, we took off.

I held onto my partner's hand. She was now sobbing. An officer who had asked if she was Mozambican had just slapped her hard on the face before she could even respond. I was terrified. I didn't know what was going to happen to me once I got to wherever they were taking us.

Still slapping people and shouting obscenities, the officers asked the guys if they were circumcised. Those who said they were not were slapped. Those who said they were circumcised were insulted.

"You got circumcised to put your @@@@ in another man's anus. You are disgusting," one officer screamed.

When we had travelled for about three minutes, the truck ran out of fuel and they took fuel from a plastic container they had. They blamed us for this, saying, "You people have sins. That's why this car is so heavy and consuming a lot of fuel."

POLICE STATION — EVENING

At the central police station, we sat on the floor and one police officer took down our names. We where harassed. Each of the officers came to see the "gays." We were paraded around. One officer identified one of our colleagues as one who had appeared a few months ago in a local tabloid. He alerted other officers and told them about the "gay boy" who was "posing as a woman," as reported in the sensationalist tabloid HMetro. They started hitting him and ridiculing him, using unprintable words. During the parade one police officer was able to identify me, since he worked with my father. He quickly shouted for others to come and see.

Once in the cells, we were separated — women and men. The men were locked up in one dirty cell with poor lighting and a dirty floor covered with urine. The women and myself were ordered to sit on a concrete bench. When all the others in the trucks had come, the men were moved from that cell to another place. We were made to stay in there.

Some people started crying. They were worried about missing curfews and about lost handbags and other valuables. Some switched on their phones to record what was happening, making sure that the police did not see them.

Once we asked the police officer to escort us to the toilet. She became rude, saying we were not serious and ordering us to behave like adults and hold our bowels.

Miles Tanhira

"We have had older women here and they can control they bowels," she said. "You are being stubborn so I will not take you." After a few minutes of begging and pleading, she gave in.

For three hours we didn't know our fate. Then we saw an SMS from someone outside, saying our lawyer was going to talk to the police. People had renewed hopes. Those were dashed when we heard a few minutes later that the lawyer had been denied access to us. We were going to spend the night in the cells.

This was a disaster. Being in the cells for three hours was painful, and the thought of the whole night or even three more days made people break down. It was Saturday of a holiday weekend [with Heroes' Day celebrated on Monday, Aug. 13]. People began to cry even worse. I was now confused and terrified, knowing that the police are notorious for detaining people, especially during such long holidays.

We were thirsty and hungry. Some women began their periods. A colleague sobbed after hearing news from home that a relative had passed on. The atmosphere grew even more somber.

POLICE STATION — MIDNIGHT TO 3 A.M.

We had nothing to do beside counting hours. Time did not seem to move. This was the longest night. By midnight we had gotten tired of sitting in the dark on the cold, wet floor.

At around 2 a.m., the police officer ordered us to remove shoes, socks, vests, bras and tights. We were to keep just one piece of clothing to cover the upper body and one for the lower body. We were going to the infamous, dehumanizing detention cells.

They took down our names, addresses and occupations, which were recorded in a huge book. Each of us got a white paper with a number written on it. The officer told us to remove any valuables, jewelry or phones for storage.

I was infuriated and scared at the same time. It was very cold, the floors were filthy yet we had to walk with bare feet. My blood began to race. Were they going to conduct body searches?

I began to shiver. My teeth were chattering. Just as we had finished deciding which piece of clothing would remain on the body, three guys from our team came in, carrying one of our members who was foaming from the mouth and shaking.

We clung to each other to keep warm. We shared one jersey which was rotated so every one could be warm for a bit. The urine on the floor, huge rats, bloody walls, dirty toilets and no lighting were enough to make one throw up with fear.

All this time, police officers would preach to us about how bad homosexuality is and that we should relocate if we want to be gay.

FROM WRONGS TO GAY RIGHTS

"It's Satanism. It's evil. It's learned at girls-only schools," they said.

As they continued talking about homosexuality, a colleague asked why they were calling us that and why they had arrested us. Because they had arrested us at GALZ, attending a meeting for gays, the officer said. This meant we were gays as well, adding that this was an offense according to Zimbabwean law.

[Editor's note: Sexual activity between men is punishable by up to a year in prison in Zimbabwe.]

POLICE STATION — 3:30 TO 6:15 A.M.

At around 3:30 a.m., two officers came in shouting obscenities and being very rude and violent. They ordered all 13 of us out of the cell, screaming that we were evil disabled people who did not know where to draw the line.

"Murikupandukira nyika mangochani evanhu, Zimbabwe inyika yakanaka hatidi izvozvo muno," they said. ("You want to overthrow the government, Zimbabwe is a beautiful country and we will not allow homosexuality here.")

A senior officer questioned the other officers: Were they sure that all of the people claiming to be men were really men and those saying they are women were indeed women?

"Have you verified these people? You can't trust them. They could be lying," he said.

They ordered us to shout our names and surnames and addresses again. They would shout, "Sex?" to which we were all supposed to say, "Female."

They demanded to have our names and addresses for the fourth time. We were each asked if we were homosexuals and why we were at a homosexual haven and how we got to know about GALZ.

The senior officer was visibly drunk. He said we were disabled people who could live in Zimbabwe only if we stopped our rotten behavior.

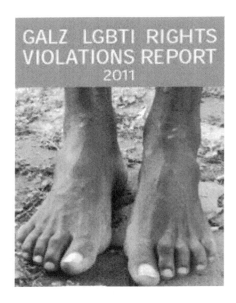

GALZ report on human rights violations

He demanded each of us to take out booklets that we allegedly had.

"Where is your constitution [for Zimbabwe] which you are making. We hear you are trying to overthrow the government. This time you will suffer," he shouted.

He threatened to report some of our colleagues so they so they could be dismissed from work.

After interrogating and hurling insults at us for about fifteen minutes while we stood in the cold, he ordered us to get back into the cells.

At around 4 a.m., the female officer came again and requested our names and addresses.

They had copies of our 2011 violations report and demanded to know who among us had participated at the GALZ meeting.

Everyone denied having been to a meeting. This infuriated the policewoman and her male colleague. They began to read the report aloud, looking for incriminating contents.

After about 30 minutes they came back into the cell and demanded to know who Tanhira was. I was scared. I was so sure they had seen my name in the report.

I answered that it was me. She did not say anything. Instead she went back to the desk and continued reading the report.

FROM WRONGS TO GAY RIGHTS

After about 15 minutes, two officers came in to take the guy who had collapsed to a hospital, since he was taking a long time to regain consciousness.

RELEASE

At around 6.15 a.m., the same senior officer who had accused us of plotting to overthrow the government gave the order for us to be released.

The junior officer, who seemed confused, wanted to know what was happening. The senior officer screamed that we should be released quickly, but they had to take down our names and addresses again before letting us out. As I was giving my name the officers questioned why I had contributed in the report [the report of LGBT-related violations that GALZ recorded in 2011] that they were holding, accusing me of making a joke of their job. It was time to go home. I couldn't be bothered. I simply refused to be drawn into that argument.

We were glad to be out of that God-forsaken place where our experience had been frustrating and scary. We had suffered harassment for close to 12 hours, only to be released without any charges or explanations. All our personal details had been recorded close to five times in a huge book by different police officers.

MEN'S SUFFERING

Once outside the police station, we shared stories of grief, pain and torture.

We learned what the guys had suffered while they were in their own cells. Some were made to slap each other and were subjected to arbitrary beatings with button sticks all night. Some had to squat, doing a frog jump, going up and down the cells' huge hall. They were ordered to lie down while police officers with their boots walked on people's backs.

The guys were also made to admit to being gay and to pair up as lovers and to imitate women's behavior. Those who refused were beaten.

WHAT'S NEXT?

A few days later we were to learn that the police were launching a man hunt for all those who had been arrested. They visited our homes and workplaces. Many were "outed" and some were dismissed from work.

For most of us, who know that the police have all our personal details. we still live in fear. After our ordeal in the cells, we know what the police are capable of.

After a second raid on the GALZ offices, they remain closed. Once again the LGBTI community has been pushed underground.

One thing's for sure: Speaking out will get us into trouble, but silence definitely will not protect us.

Gay in Cameroon:
After beatings in prison,
rejection at home

Roger Jean-Claude Mbede

By ERIC O. LEMBEMBE

JULY 12, 2012, CAMEROON — For sending amorous text messages to one of his acquaintances, Roger Jean-Claude Mbede, 33, of Cameroon has spent 16 months in prison for the crime of homosexuality.

Mbede, who is also known as Jean-Claude Roger Mbede, won provisional release on July 16 for medical treatment, but returning to his old life has proved impossible.

Most of his family has abandoned him, so he has to live with a friend. He is scheduled for surgery on July 26 for a hernia, but doesn't know how he will pay for the operation. His face is scarred from an assault in prison. And he might be returned to prison after a court hearing scheduled for Aug. 20.

FROM WRONGS TO GAY RIGHTS

In an interview on July 20, four days after his release from Kondengui Prison in the Cameroonian capital of Yaoundé, Mbede seems to have regained only his ability to smile.

"I'm back from afar," he says.

Mbede had been in prison since March 9, 2011, losing 16 months of his life for the unfortunate decision to send text messages.

He was sentenced April 28, 2011, to 36 months in prison and fined 33,000 CFA francs (about €50 or

Roger Jean-Claude Mbede

$61) for homosexuality, which under Cameroonian law is punishable by imprisonment for up to five years.

His lawyers, Alice Nkom and Michel Togué, won his provisional release this month after the court rejected more than a dozen applications.

Mbede's story begins in late 2010 when he was studying for a master's degree in the philosophy of education at the University of Central Africa in Yaoundé.

He became acquainted with a senior official serving the president of the Republic of Cameroon, he says. After four months of a friendly relationship and telephone calls, Mbede says he fell into an ambush prepared by the man, who had complained of receiving declarations of love from Mbede.

"On March 2, 2011, he called, asking me to visit him at home. To my surprise, I was greeted there by two policemen who arrested me and took me to a cell under the control of the Secretary of Defense," Mbede recalls. "For one week, I was subjected to tough interrogations without knowing what was happening. A few days later, on March 9, the public prosecutor issued a warrant and I was sent to prison the same day. After three hearings, I was sentenced," he says.

FROM WRONGS TO GAY RIGHTS

Life is hard in Kondengui Prison, especially when you're gay. "As you enter the prison, the guards hurl insults at you, such as 'faggot' and 'sorcerer.'"

Prison conditions there are difficult for everyone — not enough of the uncomfortable beds, unclean water, promiscuity, and diseases such as tuberculosis, diarrhea, and skin diseases, he says.

On top of that comes daily homophobic abuse, both verbal and physical. Inmates complained to the prison superintendent that they would not live with a "faggot" in the same room.

After suffering multiple cuts and bruises, Mbede has a scar on his brow from one of many assaults in prison.

During his time there, he received help from the Project for the Support and Assistance of Sexual Minorities, or PAEMH. The Association for the Defense of Homosexuals, or ADEFHO, brought him food and provided medical and legal aid. Amnesty International pleaded for his release.

"The PAEMH was very supportive," he says. "One of its leaders, Lamba Marc Lambert, brought me food to eat and clothes to wear. Without their assistance, I don't know what would have happened to me," he says.

He did not hear from his family after his arrest. Mbede hopes that his conviction will be overturned in an appeal scheduled for Aug. 20. Then he plans to finish his studies, find work and become independent.

"For now," he says, "I am staying at a friend's house because my family rejects me."

"My father told me that I am no longer his son," Mbede says. "If he had to choose between a madman and me, he says he would choose the madman. My sister, meanwhile, says she would prefer to have a brother who is a thief or other criminal rather than a homosexual."

As his July 26 hernia operation approaches, Mbede is worried about how he will pay for the surgery. He feels helpless and does not know where to start, he says.

As jail looms, death threats for lawyers

By COLIN STEWART

DEC. 18, 2012 — Roger Jean-Claude Mbede is trying to come to grips with the grim prospect of being sent back to prison in Cameroon for being a homosexual.

The appeal of his three-year prison sentence was denied yesterday. His attorney has 10 days to file a further appeal with the country's supreme court, even though the appeals court has given no explanation for its decision.

At the same time, lawyers in Cameroon advocating the release of defendants accused of homosexuality face death threats. Alice Nkom and Michel Togué, two Cameroon attorneys seeking Mbede's release, have been threatened in recent months and Togué received a text message threatening his children. Photos of his children leaving their school were attached to the text message.

Mbede was granted a temporary medical release in July. In a telephone interview with the Associated Press, Mbede said yesterday:

"I am going back to the dismal conditions that got me critically ill before I was temporarily released for medical reasons. I am not sure I can put up with the anti-gay attacks and harassment I underwent at the hands of fellow inmates and prison authorities on account of my perceived and unproven sexual orientation. The justice system in this country is just so unfair."

Human Rights Watch, one of many groups seeking Mbede's release, said that Mbede's case "demonstrates that basic human rights for lesbian, gay, bisexual, and transgender (LGBT) people are under assault in Cameroon." The organization urged President Paul Biya to take action, saying:

> *"Cameroon should declare a moratorium on arrests and convictions under article 347A of the Cameroonian penal code, which criminalizes 'sexual relations with a person of the same sex.' The article violates international law, including the right to privacy."*

FROM WRONGS TO GAY RIGHTS

"The appeals court decision against Roger Mbede is a blow to key human rights principles, including the right to privacy, the right to equality, and the prohibition of torture and ill-treatment," said Neela Ghoshal, researcher in the LGBT rights program at Human Rights Watch. "The decision sends a warning to LGBT Cameroonians that they risk beatings, arrests, and imprisonment simply because of their sexual orientation or gender identity."

Human Rights Watch outlined the abuse that Mbede suffered before and during his trial:

> The gendarmerie encouraged the man to whom Mbede had sent three romantic text messages to invite Mbede to his home. They arrested Mbede when he arrived there, though visiting the acquaintance's home was no crime and, in violation of Cameroonian law, the gendarmes had no warrant. They then claimed Mbede had been caught in the act of "attempted homosexuality." He was held in gendarmerie custody beyond the legal limit of 48 hours.

> After he refused to respond to interrogations, he said, he was beaten. He told Human Rights Watch: "The interrogator... called his friend, a gendarme, to beat me. The gendarme punched me in the mouth. He kept hitting me, tore my shirt. They threw away my shoes. When I went to the [prosecutor's office], I was barefoot, like a bandit."

> Under duress, Mbede says, he told gendarmes he had had three previous relationships with men, whom he was forced to name. One of the men was summoned and interrogated. The man was released after investigators concluded that he had not had sex with Mbede. However, Mbede's alleged relationship with the man still formed part of the charges.

> Mbede had no legal representation at his trial, and told Human Rights Watch that the judge shouted at him and insulted him when he tried to approach the bar to respond to the allegations against him. He was represented by a lawyer, Michel Togué, in his appeal hearing.

The organization also detailed other human rights abuses in Cameroon:

> The chief of Cameroon's police force told Human Rights Watch that article 347A is only intended to apply to those who engage in same-sex conduct publicly. But there was no evidence that the accused engaged in sexual intercourse in public in any of the recent cases that resulted in convictions.

Mbede is one of several dozen people who have been prosecuted for homosexuality in Cameroon in the last several years, beginning with a mass arrest of alleged gays at a bar in Yaoundé in 2005. Other cases are equally illustrative of human rights violations. Two men in Yaoundé were convicted of homosexuality in 2011 in a case in which the only evidence presented was that gendarmes had found a sack of condoms and lubricant in their house.

In Kribi in 2010, when intelligence officials heard that a village chief had propositioned a man, in the absence of any complaint or evidence that any crime had been committed, they set up the chief for arrest. The intelligence office's own report, seen by Human Rights Watch, says that intelligence officials convinced the man to make a date with the chief on a secluded beach. When the chief undressed at the other man's request, intelligence officials jumped out of hiding, arrested him, took pictures, and made him walk to the intelligence office stark naked. He was subsequently convicted.

In Douala in 2010, three men were arrested in a hotel lobby and charged with homosexuality because two of them had shared a room at the hotel. The case proceeded to trial, but the men fled the country before a verdict was issued.

To date, President Biya has not responded to any pleas for mercy or justice for Cameroon's LGBT community.

Death threats force attorney to flee to U.S.

By COLIN STEWART

February 18, 2013 — Lawyer Michel Togué has moved his family from Cameroon to the United States for protection after receiving death threats because of his work for gay defendants. Togué said he hopes to return to Cameroon on his own to resume that work.

"It's my duty to defend human rights and to contribute to a more tolerant Cameroon. It would be cowardly to give up," he told Agence France-Presse. AFP reported:

"Last year, Mr Togué's family started receiving threatening messages through calls, text messages and emails. They included an email which showed photographs of his

children leaving school, and phone calls asking Mr Togué's wife "which of her children she would sacrifice so her husband will give up defending homosexuals."

"Mr Togue's family left Cameroon to seek asylum in the U.S. in November, and he himself joined them in January. He said that he had received support from the French Embassy in Cameroon, but his family had gone to the US as it 'was the first to react' by giving them temporary residence.

"The family still receive threats in the US: They say they are going to kidnap my children, that they'll turn them into queers. I feel very vulnerable,' he said."

In his cell in Cameroon, awaiting trial for homosexuality

Samuel Gervais Akam

By ERIC O. LEMBEMBE

Sept. 25, 2012, CAMEROON — Arrested in June, locked up in July, Samuel Gervais Akam remains in a cell in Cameroon's overcrowded New Bell prison, awaiting trial on charges of homosexuality.

His story, told by sources close to Akam, is an ambiguous and complex tale about a married middle-aged pastry chef whose dispute with an 18-year-old boy about money and sex landed him in prison.

It started June 24 when the two met after nearly three months of dialogue on Gayromeo, a gay dating site that is popular with gay men in Cameroon. The rendezvous was between Akam, 42, of Douala, and Arold, 18, a vendor in the nearby Deido area.

When they met, everything seemed fine and Arold agreed to sex. Afterwards, when the time came to part, Akam gave Arold 2,000 FCFA (about $4) for transportation.

FROM WRONGS TO GAY RIGHTS

Arold said that was too little. Instead, he asked for 50,000 FCFA (about $100). Annoyed, Akam agreed to pay that much but not right away; he handed Arold his laptop and mobile phone as a sign of good faith.

But only a few hours later, after Arold has borrowed a motorcycle to depart, Akam followed him and caught up to him at the Ominisports Stadium in Bepanda.

"Thief!" Akam shouted. "You bandit, give me back my stuff!"

A crowd gathered. They were about to seize Arold when he cried out, "He fucked me and he did not pay. That's why I have this stuff."

The scene caught the attention of a police patrol, which took both men in for questioning and seized the laptop as evidence.

At the Bonanjo police station, investigators turned on the computer and found videos of Akam having sex with different men.

Those men are no longer in Cameroon, Akam said. Some of the videos were shot during a birthday party at his home, he said, and another one was from a visit with an expatriate couple in Kribi, Cameroon. One of the men in the scenes was his first partner, which apparently is why he kept the videos.

The PC containing "obscene and shocking" images was sealed and placed in the custody of the clerk at the High Court in Bonanjo.

Legal authorities concluded that these "images of the practice of homosexuality" were enough to merit holding Akam at the New Bell central prison, starting July 2, while he awaits his trial.

Under current law in Cameroon, the practice of homosexuality is punishable by a prison sentence as long as five years.

At present, Akam is stagnating in New Bell prison, receiving material assistance (soaps, bath oil and food) only from the gay rights groups Alternatives Cameroon and the Association for the Defence of Homosexuals (ADEFHO).

His predicament worsened in August, when his wife died after a long illness. He is downtrodden psychologically and without medical attention as he awaits his trial.

On the prosecution's side, the case is apparently still under investigation. No date has been set for Akam's trial.

For the defense, longtime gay rights defender Alice Nkom is on the case.

3 months in jail, then bail on Cameroon gay sex charge

By ERIC O. LEMBEMBE

Nov. 10, 2012 — After more than three months in prison on homosexuality charges, Samuel Gervais Akam, 42, was released Nov. 6 from the New Bell prison in Douala, Cameroon, to await his trial.

His release on bail was a victory for his attorney, Alice Nkom, a long-time defender of gay rights in Cameroon. She has been arguing for months for Akam to be released on bail on the grounds that he is in ill health and that his wife has died.

Akam was arrested June 24 on homosexuality charges after a financial dispute about sex with an 18-year-old man in the Bepanda neighborhood in Douala. A few days after the two were arrested, the youth was released. The date for Akam's trial has not been announced.

Akam, a pastry chef, almost certainly lost his job during his stay in prison. No arrangements have yet been made to assist him in returning to a normal life.

After his release from prison, Akam went to the bedside of his gravely ill daughter.

Labeled effeminate because they drink Baileys, couple appeals 5-year sentence

Jonas Singa Kumie and Franky Djome

BY ERIC O. LEMBEMBE

CAMEROON — With support from Lawyers Without Borders, two young Cameroonian men appeared in court in Yaoundé on July 20, seeking to overturn their five-year prison sentence for homosexuality, imposed in November 2011.

In addition to the five-year prison term — the maximum allowed under Cameroonian law — they were each fined 200,000 CFA francs, or about 300 euros.

The appeals court has not yet ruled on their request for release.

"I came to Yaoundé to ensure a fair trial for Jonas Singa Kumie and Franky Djome," said Saskia Ditisheim, president of Lawyers Without Borders Switzerland (ASF), which she said will send a lawyer to each trial for the crime of homosexuality in Cameroon in partnership with

Jonas Singa Kumie © Amnesty International

the local Association of Defense of Homosexuals, or ADEFHO, led by human rights attorney Alice Nkom.

In Cameroon, she said, "the social climate is increasingly dangerous for homosexuals, with numerous arrests and prosecutions."

At the July 20 appeal hearing, the judges were respectful, but spectators were not.

"I was amazed at the attitude of the judges," Ditisheim said. "Contrary to what I expected, they listened to me and even took notes. I remain confident for the future."

When the two men arrived, their rather feminine appearance caused a stir. Some in the audience were angry, some were shocked, others burst out laughing. Many taunted them with homophobic abuse.

It's already past noon, when the judges finally arrive. The hearing can begin.

FROM WRONGS TO GAY RIGHTS

Today Ditisheim represents them alongside Alice Nkom and Michel Togué, seeking provisional release for Jonas and Franky with two guarantors, Marc Lambert and Valère, who will represent them at future hearings.

"Before throwing jokes at these young people for being effeminate, remember that they have families like everyone there," argues Nkom. "In this case, there is no complaint and no victim. Why are they not set free? Because they love a person of the same sex? What did they do? Absolutely nothing! Your Honor, when you read the reasons given for these charges, you will realize that there is no flagrant crime of homosexuality in this case."

Ditisheim reminds the court of international conventions that Cameroon has ratified and that apply to this case. At that, some people in the room grumble.

"We do not want this lawyer from elsewhere. Here we are in Cameroon, the law is the law. One must respect it," someone says.

The government's attorney agrees: "Homosexuality is a crime here. The detainees have not followed the law. They are currently paying for their crime. Their two guarantors lack credibility. We cannot trust them. Besides, who says that if these young people are released, they will not leave the country to live their lives of debauchery in those countries where white men marry other men?"

The appellate judges took the matter under advisement until Aug. 3.

Jonas Singa Kumie and Franky Djome have been in jail since their arrest in late July 2011, while a third young man, arrested with them, received a provisional release because he was able to pay the fine directly.

The three men were surprised when they had sex in a vehicle on public roads in the Essos district in Yaoundé on the night of July 26 to 27, 2011.

On Nov. 22, 2011, a judge found the two men guilty and imposed the maximum sentence. He said both men were obviously effeminate because they wore wigs and had drunk Baileys, which he said is a typically feminine drink.

Abuse, victory, then pursuit by a mob

Excerpt from Amnesty International report "Republic of Cameroon: Make Human Rights a Reality" of January 2013:

In early July 2012, Amnesty International learned that Franky Ndome Ndome was, on the morning of 18 June, subjected to insults and assault by several prison guards at Kondengui prison. According to a human rights lawyer who saw him after the attack, Ndome was assaulted while returning from Wing 8 of the prison where he had gone to buy condiments to prepare his food.

A female prison guard saw him returning from Wing 8 and described him as a "pédé" (faggot). Three male prison guards joined her, threw Ndome to the ground and started kicking him as he lay on the ground. The lawyer told Amnesty International that he had been informed by Ndome that the assault lasted about 40 minutes.

The female guard got a pair of scissors and cut his hair braids while

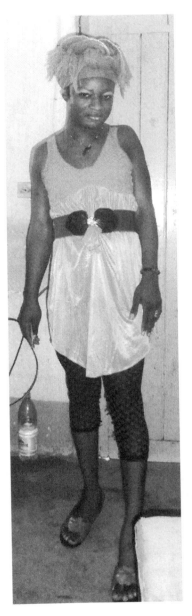

Franky Djome
© Amnesty International

pulling at them. The guards then used a chain to attach his hand to his foot and made him sit in an open drainage from the wing housing sick prisoners. Ndome told the lawyer that he remained in this position under the sun without food or water till 5pm. Ndome was reported to still be bearing scars from the beatings at the start of July.

The lawyer told Amnesty International that the authorities had failed to investigate the circumstances and reasons for the assault or to take any action against the guards.

In December 2012, Amnesty International delegates visited Kondengui prison and met the prison governor and doctor, as well as Ndome, Kimie and several other prisoners held there for homosexuality.

The prison governor told the delegates that he had no knowledge of the assault against Ndome because the latter had not reported the incident to him. Ndome explained to the delegates that he was beaten by the prison guards because he had told the female guard that he was not available to plait her hair.

He said that he told the guards that no amount of violence or other ill-treatment would make him do what he did not want or had no time to do.

Ndome and Kimie told Amnesty International's delegates that they had been arrested solely because they chose to wear women's clothes. They explained that at the time of their arrest they were not involved in any sexual act with each other or anyone else.

When asked by the delegates if they admitted to being gay, they told the delegates that their sexual preferences were a private matter and no one else's business. Moreover, they added, given the hostility of the authorities and others among Cameroonian society towards gay and lesbian individuals, it would have been foolish for them to dress in a manner that would expose them to homophobia.

They insisted that they were aestheticians and chose to dress like women from the time they met at a college in Yaoundé that trained beauticians. They told the delegates that they were aware of and were indeed subjected to prejudice and violence by prison authorities and fellow inmates but would not stop dressing the way they felt best comfortable with.

"We always felt like females from the time we were children and no one would change that", Franky said. "We have been imprisoned for dressing differently and not because we are gay", Ndome told the delegates.

On 7 January 2013, Amnesty International received the good news that the Court of Appeal in Yaoundé had just declared Ndome and Kimie innocent of the offence of homosexuality. They were released on 11 January but reportedly pursued by a group of hostile individuals, including at least one policeman, seeking to attack them. Fearing being attacked, Ndome and Kimie were in hiding in mid-January.

Meeting turns bloody
as gay-bashers invade

BY ERIC O. LEMBEMBE

CAMEROON — The attack came during a gathering to mark the end of this year's International Day Against Homophobia (IDAHO) celebrations in the Cameroonian capital of Yaoundé.

The time — about 11 p.m., Saturday, May 19. Representatives of several LGBTI organizations march one by one to the podium to discuss what the week's activities have meant to them.

Rounds of excited applause greet the speakers. The room heats up. It's time to party. A fashion show, awards presentations, songs and dances are coming up.

Outside in the courtyard about 10 men from the Nkomo neighborhood gather, having caught word of what they call "a gathering of fags."

"We must stop this," they say. "We don't want them here."

The news spreads by word of mouth through the neighborhood. Their numbers grow. Around midnight, they burst into the room. One of them hits a board against the ground.

FROM WRONGS TO GAY RIGHTS

Gay couple in Cameroon

Inside, the party atmosphere vanishes. Everyone panics. Some people run behind the podium, looking for an emergency door. Others hide under tables. The organizers call out, trying to restore calm.

Some people get away. Others not. Some are caught and beaten by the gang of gay bashers.

"Nearly two dozen people who came to the party were nearly beaten to death," says Yannick N, an organizer of the evening. "The abusers themselves said they wanted to do away with them."

Some gay men at the gathering were robbed of money, mobile phones, jewelry, identification papers, etc. Others were seized, insulted, beaten and injured, Some victims were stripped naked and forced to return home without clothes.

Gay bashers pulled gay men from taxis. They pursued young men running several thousand meters away from the party.

None of the organizers called the police because they know from experience that the police would have arrested the gay victims of the beatings rather than the gay bashers.

FROM WRONGS TO GAY RIGHTS

The gathering was organized as part of a week of IDAHO events in Yaoundé with the goal of providing a forum where young LGBTI artists could "pass along a positive message to the community." The event was supposed to include the announcement of winners of a competition for the best new work in poetry and song on the theme, "Challenging Homophobia In and Through Education." The event was also supposed to include a fashion show, songs, dances, and pastiches of famous artists, but none of those were able to take place.

Other earlier activities of IDAHO week in Yaoundé came off without major incident, including:

- A sporting event between gay and straight teams, designed to challenge preconceived ideas about gay people.
- A screening of the 2009 film "Prayers for Bobby" by American director Russell Mulcahy, which provoked a discussion about whether it is possible to change a person's sexual orientation.
- A gathering of 40 gay men who discussed methods of combating homophobia in Cameroon.
- A panel that included a teacher, a student, a journalist, a sociologist and others, who discussed ways to eliminate stigma against homosexuals.

Sponsoring organizations included Humanity First Cameroon and the Cameroonian Foundation For AIDS, or Camfaids.

Yannick N. was philosophical about the events of May 19.

"Just when we were talking about how to combat homophobia through education, we were reminded how indispensable it is that we find ways to change the deeply distorted perception of LGBTI people in Cameroonian society," he said.

Gay Pride Uganda

By RACHEL ADAMS

Walking around Kampala for the first time is confusing and disorienting. Lean-to shacks line every inch of road, motorbike taxis buzz non-stop through the tiniest gaps in traffic and for every yard of decent footpath there is a pothole twice the size. It is the end of July and I am here to cover Uganda's first ever Gay Pride. Despite making contact with the organisers back in May, I've still only had a few brief responses from them about the event.

The next few days I spend trying to get in touch with people and reading up. Only one response – an academic friend of my host who agrees to meet me for a chat about her anthropological research. It is an awkward first meeting, not helped I'm sure by my sense of urgency at wanting to pull first-hand information together. After establishing that I want to write about and, more importantly, photograph the event, she suddenly bursts out, "I mean, what happens if you lose your camera, or it gets stolen, or those pictures get into the wrong hands? Please tell me you've thought about that!"

I am taken aback – I haven't. This is Pride! I know about Ugandan tabloids hounding out LGBTI people and the murder of prominent gay activist David Kato last year, but I am also keen to carry on documenting gayness as I have been doing since 2005. I wonder how to move forward.

The next day I get a response from someone on the Beach Pride Uganda Facebook page. Joseph Kawesi says he'd like to meet up, and

The messages of Gay Pride Uganda

will bring two friends. I like Joseph even before meeting him – he has studio shots of himself on Facebook and their apparent innocence beguiles me.

Gently posing, playing a guitar and doffing his cap to the camera this man has put pictures of himself on an open-access page, knowing that in doing so he could be identified and attacked by members of the public or the police. We set a time for later that day and when they arrive we chat.

FROM WRONGS TO GAY RIGHTS

Their organisation – Youth on Rock Foundation – is one of around 40 NGOs in Uganda working on LGBTI issues. Their aim is to support the most disadvantaged minorities in the slums of Kampala and they are based in Bwaise, near to where I am staying. Sensing that they want me to see the conditions they are trying to improve, I suggest we go directly there. Again, I am shocked. The network of concrete shacks they live in is interwoven with open drains and rotting piles of rubbish.

When we get to the one-room shack they all share they tell me about their lives – Morgan lost his job as a teacher after coming out; Bad Black, a trans woman, was kicked out of school and has contracted HIV from one of her sex work clients.

Later that evening they take me to their local bar, owned by a professional boxer. They feel safe there and say it's one of only a handful of places in the city they can use and, just as importantly, afford. Their friend Jay joins us after his basketball match, and tells me he lost his scholarship from university after they found out he was gay. Now unable to finish his education, he says he feels hopeless and lost.

The following week I talk to people at a hospital's LGBTI-friendly STD clinic, I do some more pictures with Black, Joseph and Morgan and I go to the Freedom to Roam Uganda office (a well-established lesbian organisation running the Pride event) to get my Pride ticket.

Hidden behind metal gates on the outskirts of Kampala, it is a safe place for people like Stosh, who was not only correctively raped as a teenager, but also hounded out of her community and forced to live in hiding because she is gay.

The anthropologist is there, and tells me about her friends in the community who are being harassed. I find it difficult to navigate the conversation, sensing that she is indirectly warning me off covering the event. Two women, Didi and Bigi, come out, and I ask them about photos.

"What exactly are you going to do with them?" they say.

"I'll be sending them out to the international newspapers, and maybe using them for a longer documentary project," I reply.

FROM WRONGS TO GAY RIGHTS

Celebrating Gay Pride in Uganda.

Bigi raises her voice: "You've got to understand that these people will say, 'Yes, take my photo,' but they don't realise what will happen afterwards. The pictures will be all over the Web and they're not even out to their families. We've had problems before with journalists coming over, saying they're going to write a story and then they just publish what they want. You have to get people's permission, and you have to understand that these people's lives are in danger."

I'm just about to say "OK," when a woman walks into the office and says, "Hi, my name is Sophia. I'm a photographer from Tunisia..." Bigi sighs in exasperation.

As Pride weekend approaches, I hear conflicting information from everyone – that police know about the event, that they don't, that it will be safe, that it won't.

On the opening night, at a gay-friendly hotel still under construction, brochures are handed out with a verbal proviso: "Don't drop these programmes or lose them." I stow mine away carefully.

The night is the first of the "Kuchu Film Festival" and, after watching some international shorts and the "Call Me Kuchu" documentary about

FROM WRONGS TO GAY RIGHTS

Kato, there are some rousing speeches and a rendition of the group's anthem, "LGBTI: Children of the Rainbow Flag."

Kasha, the founder of FARUG and the brains behind Pride, reads from her brochure: "We are not going to wait for the 'traditional' street pride march. Instead, we are gonna have BEACH PRIDE in Uganda... If you can be proud of who you are alone, why not join others and celebrate your pride together?"

She tells me that the event is for her and her friends, and the march is being held in a public park in Entebbe, 35 kilometers from Kampala, on Saturday, not Sunday, when the park will be less busy. They have permission to erect a stage on the shores of Lake Victoria, but had to say it was for Kasha's birthday. I am told they asked for police protection but it was refused.

Later that night, Morgan introduces me to an activist called Clare who works for the Civil Society Coalition on Human Rights and Constitutional Law. She has just come from a four-hour meeting with the Inspector General of Police, a "brilliant man," she says, who "listens to people's grievances." I am surprised.

"That's incredible!" I say, delighted that this "ear to the President" is listening. He told Clare that the community "should carry out research about how people become gay and educate the public. He also said he is willing to learn more about these issues."

I speak to Bishop Christopher Senyonjo, the Ugandan LGBTI community's pastor who went into temporary exile in the US after receiving death threats and who was ousted from the Ugandan Anglican Church after 24 years for his support of the LGBTI community.

Bearing in mind the importance of religion to Ugandan society, and the Ugandan government's accusation that homosexuality is a Western concept and un-African, I want to know whether secular activism can work here.

"'You cannot forget religion here, but what you need is sensitisation. Some religious people understand. That is what I'm trying to do – have dialogue. Talk about human sexuality. Along with other rights," he says.

FROM WRONGS TO GAY RIGHTS

"Secular activism is needed, and a lot of education. People need education whether they are religious or not. Teaching, education, advocacy is very important."

I ask whether it is difficult for him to work now that the church has ex-communicated him.

"I go to the church; people don't want to know me but I talk to them. My church doesn't like me to preach here but I have continued to because faith seeks understanding. God has given us our reasoning to use. These people are real. How can they be denied their reality?"

In the last year since Kato was killed have you sensed any kind of change?

"I think people have come to understand that homosexuality is real, that you don't choose it like you choose smoking. It is part of our work to educate. With education, things will change."

It is comforting to meet someone religiously pro-gay, but the following day I ask a member of the group if she has Simon Lokodo's number – Uganda's Minister for Ethics and Integrity.

"You want to speak to that crazy man?" she texts. After deliberating about what to ask the man responsible for banning 38 NGOs on the basis that they promote homosexuality, I phone him. He would rather conduct the interview in person, so he tells me where to go and I get on a boda-boda, or bicycle taxi.

It's a strange sensation, waiting to meet the person who has the power to deport you for being morally unsound. We talk for about 40 minutes. He gives his justification for June's raid on an NGO meeting:

"A month and half ago we did an investigation on NGOs who were mixing positive things with things which we call in Uganda bad. We realised that a number of them were actually raising funds from abroad in the guise of promoting humanitarian concerns. They were also going around implanting in the minds of small children and persons below 18 attitudes of perverted, disoriented feelings in their sexual expressions. In other words, they were supportive of homosexuality and lesbianism, which is not permitted in Uganda. The constitution is clear about this, that marriage between persons of the same sex, relations between persons of the same sex, is prohibited and punishable in aggravated cases with life imprisonment.

"So we found that these NGOs were out of order and we have requested the Ministry of Internal Affairs to reduce them so they don't go around giving a bad attitude, a bad spirit, a bad culture which will destroy this country's morale. Just imagine if tomorrow every Ugandan accepted homosexuality."

There is a pause. I ask, "What would happen?"

Another pause.

"We would cease to be. Sex is for procreation. In time there will be a build-up of homosexuals. A lot of young people will opt for that because it will put in [sic] sex as pleasure, not child bearing. Some people spend hours doing nothing but disturbing themselves. It's meaningless. Sexual pleasure for what?"

I notice that Lokodo isn't wearing a wedding ring and ask him if he is married. He hands me his business card, which reads "Hon. Rev. Fr. Simon Lokodo" and he tells me that before he went into politics he was ordained as a priest and took vows of celibacy.

I'm curious as to who his advisors are on LGBTI rights. He doesn't seem to understand the question so I ask him where he gets his information on homosexuality. He tells me that people come to his office because they are afraid of going to the public hospitals. Four or five people come a day to tell them about the "abuse" they have suffered.

I ask if he thinks people are born gay or if they become homosexual, and he says, "What I know [is] that, born or become, it is a perversion. I know it is an ailment. It is a sickness. It is not a status to be applauded. I am told that if a child is in a mother's womb and there are situations that are negative that person will come out with a negative attitude towards that gender."

Having heard enough, I switch off the dictaphone and he asks me what my opinion is. I say that I think that people should be allowed to live freely, to which he replies, "So you think that if people want to go round killing each other they should be allowed to? You know, if you are one of those people I would take you straight to the airport." I don't tell him I'm gay because I don't want to miss Pride the next day.

That night's agenda includes some more films and a well-attended fashion show, the models confidently strutting their stuff down a specially made catwalk in t-shirts emblazoned with slogans: "The closet is for clothes – come out, come out wherever you are," "My sexual preference is often" and my favourite: "Straight – so is spaghetti 'til you heat it up." I go home fairly early to get ready for the next day.

At 10 a.m. outside the National Theatre in town, a few people are waiting for the pre-booked coach to take them to Entebbe. No one is completely sure where we are going. Morgan, Black and Joseph greet me, and we get on the yellow bus.

Black gets out her compact on the seat in front of me and deftly applies bubblegum pink eyeshadow and lip gloss to her dark skin. She has her favourite red bra and a sarong to change into. The bus gradually fills up, and on the way we stop at a garage. Clare and I chat outside the bus and I notice her pillar-box red t-shirt which says in capital letters, "Some People Are Gay – Get Over It." People look and stare, some smile, some look confused. We carry on.

On arrival, I see barbecues have been set up. Men in sarongs and rainbow flags add charcoal and cut chips out of bins full of potatoes. There is a trestle-table bar with free beer and pop, and the stage is set up on the shore of the lake. A VIP gazebo is festooned with rainbow ribbons and the DJs blast tunes from big speakers. A single table with Pride t-shirts for sale sits between the eating area and the stage.

It feels festive, and fairly private. Peanut sellers wander around amiably, and when I ask them about the rainbow flags, they say they're pretty. I assume they don't recognise the significance. While we are waiting for the parade to start, I ask Clare what would happen if they ran it down Kampala Road in the city centre.

"We would be stoned to death."

"And I say that with conviction," she adds.

Families and children follow the Pride parade

I notice a line of people not with our group standing beyond the stage further along the beach and I watch them make their way in groups of two and three into the water. They are being baptised.

Maurice Tomlinson of Jamaica, a legal advisor with AIDS-Free World, has been invited to act as the event's Grand Marshal. He climbs onto the back of a pick-up truck with Ugandan LGBTI activist and spokesperson Frank Mugisha, a few others and myself. We drive along the path to a field where people have started to dress up. Rainbow flags, stickers, glitter and placards are gradually brought out until the group of around 50 people is decorated in unmistakable gayness. Four local men and women with babies watch silently.

The parade starts. Music blasts from the speakers on the truck and Maurice leads with a placard that reads, "Gay And African – Not A Choice." Gradually the parade gathers momentum and before long all I can see are faces ecstatic with what I can only assume is a feeling of freedom. Dancing becomes wilder and jubilant shrieks reach a crescendo. The scene is one of blissful childlike joy on a background of natural beauty, rainbow colours flitting around in gleeful high visibility. Finally I've found the beauty I've been wanting to photograph.

FROM WRONGS TO GAY RIGHTS

As the parade makes its way round the gardens, a few onlookers gather and soon a group of small children is following the parade, holding hands with some of the participants, unaware of the event's historical significance. As we make our way back to the stage area, people carry on dancing and food is handed out, including to members of the public who have joined to watch. I wander around taking a few more snaps and ask Frank what he has just experienced.

"My life right now is Pride itself, because I'm very visible. The police officers know my name. I was worried about the media sneaking and taking photos and we are used to the police coming, but we said we'll be strong and we won't let that stop us," he says.

Suddenly Morgan approaches me and takes me to the top of the hill. "The police are here," he whispers. I look around. There are a few men in combats and a white truck stationed near the path. I wander back towards Morgan, eating with one hand and holding my camera with the other.

A man in a white t-shirt and baseball cap comes up to me. He asks what I'm doing there. I say 'Nothing,' and carry on eating. He asks me who I am, where I'm from. He keeps on questioning me, enough for me to ask him who he is. He gets out some ID from his pocket and flashes it in my face like a TV cop. I notice an official-looking symbol and the name Ivan.

He asks to see my ID. I worry. I go to the bus and get my purse. It has a photocopy of my passport in it so I get it out and hand it over. He slaps it in irritation and asks what I'm doing here in Uganda. I say I'm on holiday. He asks when I arrived, and I say two weeks ago. He asks for my visa. I say it's in my passport back at my accommodation.

He is becoming increasingly aggressive. I say I can go and get my visa and bring it to the police station if he would like. He tells me he is arresting me so I ask why. No response. After a few minutes a few of the group start to gather round and ask what is going on. I say I am being arrested but I don't know why. There is more aggression and various points of view, but mainly, people tell me not to worry, they will go with me to the station. Someone takes my camera and I give my spare memory cards to a man called Michael to hide. Dusk is falling.

FROM WRONGS TO GAY RIGHTS

I start to get a little nervous as I see two trucks full of male officers. I say I'm not going to the station alone in one of those trucks. Someone says they will insist on a female officer (to bide time, they tell me) and there is more arguing, and my repeated question: "Why are you arresting me?" Ivan never gives a reason. I ask to see his ID again and he refuses to show it. We all ask several times, and he refuses. Despite arguing and trying to persuade this man for about half an hour, he won't back down. At one point he pushes me in frustration.

A female police officer arrives, and when the group tries to hold me back, she hits them with her baton. She bustles me off, and I ask her why I'm being arrested. "Homosexuality is illegal in Uganda," she whispers conspiratorially. When we get to the police motorbikes, I tell them I'm not getting on without a helmet. The driver gives me his. My last pathetic attempt to avoid being taken to the station has failed. Jay has insisted they let him get on the other bike and we are driven slowly to the station just beyond the entrance to the park. All I have on me is my purse and my dead phone.

On arrival at the station. we are told to sit down on a bench facing a man with a big logbook. He writes someone's details down and Jay whispers to me not to mention the camera at all. The South African writer who has been documenting the event sits down on the bench next to me and starts to write something. She is asked who brought her. She says she doesn't know and then starts to get irate, eventually getting into a scuffle with the female officer, who again resorts to using her baton. Ivan comes and sits down to give his statement. The man with the register then tells Ivan to go upstairs and he takes my photocopied passport. He asks why I'm here and when I'm leaving. I remember I have my return plane ticket in my purse, so I give him that too.

I see one of the performers, Beyondy, behind me and because I have heard that she has been beaten I ask her if she's OK. She nods, just, and gets ready to leave. Kasha and Frank arrive at the desk and tell me not to say anything, that I haven't done anything wrong, and that they can't arrest me.

After a while I ask if it's OK to go and smoke a cigarette. Outside a couple of plain clothes police officers tell me to move to the side with my "unhealthy habit." I do. More of the LGBTI group have arrived as well as Maurice. A girl hugs me and I see a camera flash go off.

FROM WRONGS TO GAY RIGHTS

"It's funny when the journalist becomes the story." Maurice grins, and he steps in front of me. Others in the group hug each other and wave their rainbow flags in front of the photographer provocatively while he snaps away. Kasha entertains the officers with some break-dancing. They know her by name.

Then out of nowhere a buff man with a cockney accent taps me on the shoulder and says with authority, "Rachel, I'm Simon. British military. Are you ok?" I say I'm fine, and he says "I've come to get you out of here." My photocopy and my ticket are handed round to a few different people and amidst the confusion I ask him who he is.

"Don't worry, someone made a call and pulled in a few favours. British military, that's all you need to know."

It becomes apparent that Ivan is a soldier, not a police officer, and that someone from the military phoned Simon to get me out of there before the British Consul could be informed.

They don't know that Frank has already phoned them, and that Clare has called the Inspector General, who has told the station to let everyone go. Maurice – who was also detained with some others – exclaims that this is all "absolutely ridiculous" and that the police are making fools of themselves.

Then it's over. Simon takes me and Jackie to his van, and asks if we need a lift. Jackie says thanks, but that we should all stick together. We are driven from the police station back to Kampala by Robert, head of the LGBTI group's security team.

On Sunday evening there is the closing "hangover" party. We spend the night chatting, drinking, dancing and celebrating the fact the Uganda has just had its first Gay Pride event.

On Monday I am keen to speak to Beyondy, the trans performer who was arrested and beaten. She should be at college but is too shaken to go. She tells me that on Saturday afternoon she was about to go on stage to perform when she and the group saw the police and drove off.

The police chased them to the garden gates, which she thinks were

Relaxing on a rainbow flag in Uganda

locked in advance. She was dragged out of the car by her hair and held by three officers while one beat her. Her friends locked themselves inside the car. Park security guards and a small group of people watched.

She shows me where they pulled her hair out, the mark on the inside of her lip and the scratches on her arm. She says she wants the police officers dealt with, but she can't go public. She is not out to her family. She says she is scared: "If the police can do this to me, what will the public do?"

Later on I get the Inspector General's number and call him, giving my name and saying that I was arrested on Saturday night. He says he spoke to the police, who told him that the public were concerned having seen "a group of girls fondling and kissing each other in public." I ask if that is illegal, and he says no, but that Uganda has laws against indecent behaviour. He says the police were also told there was a gay wedding going on. (In fact, a gay wedding did take place in Kampala that night, but it went undisturbed by police.)

He tells me he ordered everyone at the police station to be released. He gives me the number of the chief of police, Andrew Kawesi. He says that members of the public were concerned that people were behaving in a "scandalous" way "in front of young children." He says he told his officers to go to the park and, if it was true, then the offenders were to be "told our concerns, and let go." I tell him that one of the group was badly beaten. Kawesi apologises and says, 'We will make a public apology. If they used excessive force, we are very sorry." He continues, "The beach is open to all people and some of these rights have not been fully institutionalised. The only mistake they could have made is using excessive force."

Although the Ugandan government criminalises homosexuality, David Bahati's "Kill the Gays" bill is a proposed bill only. Simon Lokodo will be in court in September, charged with unconstitutional closure of workshops. U.S. Secretary of State Hillary Clinton awarded Clare, Frank and other members of the Coalition an award for Human Rights work the day before Pride.

The fact that four days of Pride events took place is a huge achievement and an admirable show of bravery for all those involved because widespread evangelical and institutionalised homophobia informs society to the point that many LGBTI people in Uganda live in constant fear of persecution. A few days after Pride, as I watch pictures being posted online and gushing comments of "We did it!" I feel a sense of relief that the aftermath of the event is on the whole positive. Kasha notes that she has been receiving "funny phone calls," but I'm thrilled to read that next year the march will start from the police station. I hope I can go.

[Editor's note: After the 2012 Gay Pride event, the struggles of LGBT people in Uganda continued, of course. The Anti-Homosexuality Bill proposed by member of parliament David Bahati remained a source of controversy, but it had not yet been acted up before the parliamentary session ended in December. Many people expect it to pass in 2013. LGBT activists' court case against ethics minister Simon Lokodo for shutting down their workshops has been continued into 2013. Joseph Kawesi of the Youth on Rock Foundation was arrested on homosexuality charges on Dec. 31, 2012, and was detained for several days. After his release, he and several colleagues went into hiding for their own protection and waited to hear whether the charges against them would be pursued or dropped.]

For assaulted trans woman, Uganda medical care must be anonymous

By ANDY KOPSA and CLARE BYARUGABA

A Day in Kampala: a trans-woman is viciously assaulted in a hate crime, the police won't readily help, and there's little hope for justice. This is just one story of just one day of paying the price of being LGBTI in Uganda.

We were in Clare's car on our way to a hospital we can't talk about to see a doctor we can't mention to treat a person who – still – in Uganda doesn't exist.

Clare drove honking and weaving – an expert – through the choking Kampala traffic. Across her dashboard was a rainbow sticker and flag, and the flags of both Uganda and the United States. Ruth was hanging on the passenger side; Beyonce, Mich and I crammed into the back.

After some time we reached the hospital that a diplomat had directed Beyonce to. She – Beyonce – had spoken to the official earlier that day to make the necessary arrangements. When we pulled into the hospital's driveway, three representatives of a foreign government were waiting in an SUV.

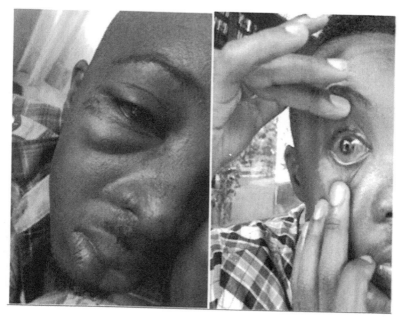

Mich two days after she was beaten, on left, and four days afterward, at right.

We got out and walked over to meet Beyonce's contact. I introduced myself as a journalist from the US. The official immediately stopped and turned to look at me. She was clearly displeased — beyond that really; she looked worried. Beyonce hadn't told her I would be along, but Beyonce wasn't worried about me; she was just looking to get Mich help.

Visibly upset, pacing, the official told me my being there could put Mich and Beyonce in jeopardy. She was angry. I apologized, but for what I wasn't entirely sure. In fact, she continued, my being there as a member of the press could put the "entire network and relationship with the hospital in jeopardy."

The relationship they had groomed with the facility was a long time in the making. This clandestine series of phone calls, pick ups, drop offs and assists carefully was calculated by another government that cannot talk of their involvement in any of this openly. I consented – promised the diplomat repeatedly – to stay outside. I had to swear not mention the hospital, doctor or foreign agency involved. This is how a transsexual who is brutally assaulted in a hate crime gets medical attention in Uganda, if they are lucky enough to be treated.

* * *

On Tuesday, Mich had met a friend at a fresh, new-looking bar on the outskirts of Kampala. It was warm as usual and Mich looked forward to seeing her friend. But what happened next was not expected. Mich's friend had invited another friend to the club, a friend she didn't know. After some chatting, that man began taunting Mich, saying, "You look like my girlfriend, you have a figure like a woman, I don't like the way you look!"

Then he brutally beat her. It happened quickly, Mich thought maybe he was just joking around when he was taunting her. She did not expect that this man, whom she had never met before, whom she had not offended at all, would get violent. But he started the assault in the open courtyard of the club. He pushed Mich to the concrete, started to thump her face mercilessly, at the same time holding her by the throat with an intention of strangling her to death. Friends of his joined in the beating, kicking her in the ribs and chest.

Mich was born in the wrong body – that of a boy — and her assailant knew it. He hated and almost killed her for it.

Mich asserts that what saved her was her insistent screaming for help, to which the askari (or guard) responded by pulling her away from the attackers. And then it was over. Mich got away, found a boda-boda bicycle taxi and escaped to a friend's house.

Although the attack took place on a Tuesday, Mich didn't report the beating until Thursday – and only after her friend and fellow transgender woman, Beyonce, found out the beating had occurred.

* * *

The stigma the LGBTI community in Uganda faces hasn't gone away. Simply because the infamous Bahati bill met with a tremendous Western backlash doesn't mean there are human rights for all in this country. No, human rights for all doesn't apply in Uganda.

FROM WRONGS TO GAY RIGHTS

Clare found out about the beating as part of her job. As the co-coordinator for Uganda's Civil Society Coalition on Human Rights and Constitutional Law, she deals with the brutality, discrimination and inequality that the LGBT community in Uganda faces every day.

When she accompanied Mich to Old Kampala Police Station, the first question the officer asked was "Is this a boy or a girl?"

Clare couldn't contain herself. She yelled at the officer, "What kind of question is this! What kind of professionalism is this?" But as an open LGBT community leader in Uganda, she must be careful. The police are not too welcoming to her community.

* * *

Beyonce talked to me as we waited for word on taking Mich to a hospital. She's "a little nervous," she said.

"It's like through here," Mich said, gesturing around her neck where she had been choked, "and right through here," motioning with her fingers across her rib cage. She had already seen a doctor, but her pain was worsening and it was time to go to that unnamed hospital.

You have to be careful," Beyonce said, "you have to find 'friendly' doctors at 'friendly' hospitals if you are a trans-woman."

Beyonce couldn't stop fidgeting, readjusting herself in her seat, rearranging her purse on the table, then on her lap, then back on the table.

"I haven't been able to sleep because I will dream that people are after me. When she [Mich] had her trauma, I remembered my trauma and I can't sleep and I can't eat," Beyonce said.

She was beaten into a coma at a club for not "dressing like a man.". She was dragged from the toilet and thrown into the street. A friend of hers said a bouncer yelled at her, telling her to "go home and put on men's shoes."

Because of that beating, she thrust herself into activism, founding Transgender Equality Uganda (TEU).

* * *

Beyonce talks about the specific needs of the male-to-female transsexual compared to the LGB population.

"We are sex workers, a lot of us, and that is all people see. It is like we are the awful face of LGBT so we are stigmatized by gay men too. It is lesbians and trans women that are the worst of the worst in the community's eyes."

"They don't even know about transphobia, because [to them] we don't exist. Unless we are on papers, we aren't humans." Beyonce says. "To the government, we don't exist. If we don't exist, how do we educate people about us?"

* * *

We were on our way to the bar now, driving again, Clare honking and the music loud. We had to find witnesses to the beating.

The cops don't do that kind of work here. They don't investigate — certainly not an attack on an LGBTI person, and not for a crime like a transphobic or a homophobic attack — which the entire police force may not be informed about because such crimes don't exist in the crime book.

Mich would have to become her own detective, find her own proof — present some sort of evidence beyond a bloodied and beaten face.

Mich's friend who invited her out for drinks refused to testify on her behalf. He was afraid.

Clare tried to talk with him on the phone, telling the friend he didn't have to identify himself. He could just give his statement to the police anonymously. But he wouldn't.

FROM WRONGS TO GAY RIGHTS

Clare and Mich outside the bar where Mich was beaten

So it was up to them – Ruth jokingly said that our investigation felt a little like "mob justice." And she's right, it did. But the fact is that there is no one else to do the work, because the police won't do it in most LGBTI hate crime cases.

A song that Beyonce loves came on the radio as we were driving through town. She squealed with her arms raised: "This reminds me of Cape Town. Everyone is so free!"

"I just love Calcutta. In Calcutta they don't hate little girls who are born little boys." She had been to a conference there recently as a result of her advocacy.

But, although she loves other places where she can be herself more easily, she doesn't want to leave. None of them wants to leave Uganda.

FROM WRONGS TO GAY RIGHTS

Despite the revival of the infamous Bahati Bill (also known as the "Kill the Gays" bill), despite proposed anti-gay amendments to the penal code, despite Ethics Minister Simon Lokodo's crusade against "pro gay" NGOs and LGBT workshops, they stay.

This is our fight as Ugandans, this is our country, they say. We can't run away because of what we go through. As advocates, we have to help bring about change, a change that was set into motion because an activist one day said, "Enough is enough. We need to break the silence."

* * *

At the bar, Beyonce, Clare and Mich talked to a young waitress who insisted she didn't know anything about anything that happened that night.

No one would speak about the beating. The security guard told us he only speaks Rwandese, though our group wasn't buying that line from him.

"He doesn't speak Lugandan? He doesn't speak English? He doesn't even speak Swahili?," Beyonce said. "He's lying." Chances are she is right.

Mich got the same cold shoulder inside. The bar owner said the staff that was working that night – the night Mich was beaten in public – weren't working for her anymore. "We have new staff," she told Mich and Clare as they stood at the counter. Clare looked at her incredulously. "You have new staff? This was just Tuesday."

Mich pleaded, "It was around 11:00. We were here and here." She pointed to different locations in the bar. But the owner wouldn't budge. But she did say the person she thought Mich was looking for "left the country." And then nothing more.

A feeling of dejection and a sense of exhaustion dropped like a ton of bricks. Like the feeling you get when you are expecting that amazing phone call from that particular boy or when you hope for a special Christmas gift; but then the call doesn't come and the present isn't under the tree – only the stakes are much higher than a broken heart or an unfulfilled wish. We all decided it was time to leave.

The group began to see the hopelessness of trying to find a witness who would come to police as a witness to what happened on that fateful night. Clare's LGBT legal committee had tried to push the issue further, but the lack of a willing witness hindered its progress. Mich had failed to find a job because of stigma about how she looks, so her financial constraints made pursuit of the case difficult.

We tried to secure an arrest warrant that would allow the assailant to be arrested on sight, but who would sit at the bar everyday to wait for him when he might never show up again? Mich kept pondering those questions. Frustrated, she was considering giving up the case and returning home to western Uganda.

Clare and Mich sat on the hood of Clare's car at the bar where the beating took place. We were getting ready to leave as the reality that no one would come forward as a witness sank in.

* * *

The U.S. Federal Bureau of Investigation defines a hate crime as "a criminal offense committed against a person, property, or society that is motivated, in whole or in part, by the offender's bias against a race, religion, disability, sexual orientation, or ethnicity/national origin."

The only way a "hate crime" ends up in the news in Kampala is if there is a trashy photo of a beat-up trans-woman or LGBT person that can be splashed across the front page of some tabloid. That kind of shock value is a good sell.

Homophobia, transphobia and inexplicable hatred of LGBTI persons in Uganda are real. Just because it doesn't make the front cover of Western publications these days doesn't change that fact.

* * *

When I interviewed Lokodo, the ethics minister, he told me point-blank, "Homosexuality is a sickness. They must be contained and away from society." This opinion is in "lock step" with that of First Lady Janet Museveni, he said.

As Clare told me toward the end of our ride, "This is what we deal with every day. We go to bed with it. We wake up with it. This is what it is like to be an LGBT person in Uganda. You cannot underestimate someone pointing at you or taunting you. You have to read between the lines and realize it as a potential threat to your life, and you have to ensure your safety."

HIV-positive activist to Uganda: Stop impeding AIDS battle

By COLIN STEWART

Ugandan legislators are obstructing the country's fight against AIDS, says HIV-positive human rights activist Maxensia Nakibuuka of Uganda.

People are being scared away from HIV treatment by the parliament's focus on the so-called "Kill the Gays" bill and a less publicized bill to jail HIV-positive people who have sex without disclosing their infection, Nakibuuka says.

"Our country spearheaded the advocacy on HIV and AIDS in the early 90s, but now the virus is rising because there is reduced education, sensitization and support, especially to those at risk," she said in a video supporting the work of the Global Fund Against AIDS, Tuberculosis and Malaria.

Nakibuuka, who founded and runs the Lungujja Community Health Caring Organisation in Kampala, is an HIV-positive mother of four and a widow for the past 16 years, since her husband died of AIDS.

*Maxensia Nakibuuka: Stop scaring people
away from HIV tests and treatment*

In Uganda, the overall HIV infection rate grew from 6.4 percent in 2005 to 7.3 percent in 2012. The estimated rate for men having sex with men is 12.4 to 13.7 percent.

Under current Ugandan law, the punishment for homosexual activity is life imprisonment. Health centers serving that population often work in secret to avoid harassment.

In her video, Nakibuuka says that after her husband's death in 1999, she lost her job because of stigmatization. She was in desperate straits until the Kamwokya Christian Caring Community, the Global Fund and the U.S. Pepfar Fund offered treatment, assistance, and counseling for her and her family.

FROM WRONGS TO GAY RIGHTS

The following paragraphs are excerpts from her video:

"I was down, sickly and had lost hope, even to bring up my children.

"In 2005, I had no job, I had no food for my children, I had no income, I was sick.

"It was the Pepfar Fund and the Global Fund, through Kamwokya Christian Caring Community, that I started [antiretroviral (ARV) drugs] in 2006.

"I chose to be part of the activism to end HIV and I offered my own premises to have my own clinic that is offering treatment, mobilizes women and men and youth to do care-giving from house to house, follow up to patients who are on treatment, advise on nutrition, and other support services. And for the past six years, my 56 volunteer care-givers have volunteered to do this.

"If we had ARVs at the time I lost my husband, he wouldn't have died.

"I thank God that I had access to treatment and now I am becoming so strong. "When you are infected by HIV and AIDS, it's not only drugs that you need to live. You need support, you need care, you need counseling, you need food, you need every kind of support.

'And unfortunately we are not getting this support. Many lives have been lost."

Anti-TB drugs are in short supply in Uganda, she said, and politicians are making matters worse.

"In parliament, we have two controversial bills — the HIV bill and the anti-gay bill. As we mobilize everybody to come in voluntarily for tests, now we have these legislators who are sitting down and making these bills, scaring people away, including myself.

"Because if an HIV bill is saying that whoever who will be found positive will be put into jail, I will be the first person, because I am positive. Is this how the government should support us?

"No one has ever knelt down to God to get HIV. What about the younger children who get HIV transmitted from their mothers? What about the young girls who are raped? What about the sex workers on the streets? Should we hold them as criminals?

"We need to think again about how people catch HIV and AIDS.

"I call upon my government first to support its own people. Give us the support we need. Bring the drugs. Put it at every point that is very accessible for everybody to reach. Educate the people that the virus is still with us."

"And we still pray to the Global Fund to give us more support, so we can kick AIDS out of the whole world altogether."

GLIMPSES

Ghana:
Tough life for gays

Excerpts from a description of gay life in Ghana. From GayGhana.org:

Stigma

There is a lot of stigma towards gay men and lesbians living in Ghana. ... We are not criminals. We are not evil. We are not devils....

I was approached by a friend who has been asked why he walks or talks with me. People see him with me and think because of that, he is evil and will never go to heaven; because gays are evil men.

I was evicted from my first room that I rented, because they said no woman visits me and that means I am gay.

I was beaten by a man who thought I had no right to reply to his wife when she insulted me for being gay, because gays are "nothing." He said, "Who are you? Homosexual talking to my wife like that?"

Violence

Gays / homosexuals in Ghana are living in the state of fear. ... We are beaten, even when we attend funerals, by young men who think being gay is foolish. We are attacked and robbed and all people say to us is, "What where you doing there by that time and who invited you there?"

Human rights

Gays are not recognized in Ghana. ... Even though the constitution of Ghana gives everyone the right to association, gay men can't meet to discuss issues that affect them in Ghana since it is believed that gays are not humans.

Health care

Gay men don't go to the hospitals for treatment especially if it is a sexually transmitted disease. Most of these diseases, you are asked to bring with you your sexual partner before treatment. Gay sex has been described as criminal, so most men come home and forget the hospital and fall on friends for help.

Law

Even though the criminal code of Ghana has no clear-cut definition of homosexuality or gay life style, the lawyer uses a portion that talks about "unnatural sex" which is sex with an animal.

[Editor's note: Under Ghanaian law, consensual sex "in an unnatural manner" is a misdemeanor.]

HIV-AIDS prevention

Even though there are lots and lots of HIV prevention going on in Ghana, the LGBT has been left out. The is no prevention or awareness targeting this community and this has caused lots of damage to us. ...

[Editor's note: Ghana's overall HIV infection rate is estimated at 1.8 percent, but it's 25 percent for men who have sex with men.]

.

Iraq:
Death trap for gay men

In early 2012, death squads unopposed by the Iraqi government repeatedly attacked gay Iraqis and those who had adopted goth-like "emo" styles. Human rights groups protested the deaths of dozens of gay and "emo" Iraqis.

Then, in mid-2012, the BBC reported on a new aspect of the peril. A report by Natalia Antelava, titled "Witch-hunt in Iraq," revealed that police and the army were involved in raping and killing gay men. Militias that operate death squads were getting intelligence about the identities of sexual minorities from the Ministry of the Interior, the BBC said.

In a safe house at an undisclosed location in Iraq, run by an undisclosed human rights organization, Antelava interviewed three gay men who described why they sought protection. All three reported receiving death threats.

- Ahmed had not left the room for over two months. He was threatened by his immediate family and people from his neighborhood. With the post-war return of relative stability to Iraq, Ahmed said, "Now they have nothing to do but to look for gays to kill them."

- "Nancy," a transgender male-to-female woman, said she was raped by nine men at a security checkpoint.
- Allou said he too was raped. "The threat is much bigger now than before. It's the militias, the police, the government who are going after us," he said.

Qais, a former policeman who is gay himself, said he quit his job because he was ordered to focus on tracking down gays.

"In 2007, 2007, 2008 we were busy fighting terrorism. We didn't pay attention to gays. On top of it, the Iraqi government had to respect the rule of law more when the Americans and the British were here. But now they have a lot of free time and the police are going after gays," he said.

Russia:
Timeline of gay rights
and gay repression

1993: Repeal of Russian law that provided for prison sentences of up to five years for male homosexual activity.

1999: Homosexuality removed from Russia's official list of mental illnesses.

2001: Russian Ministry of Health prohibits blood donations from homosexuals, drug addicts and prostitutes.

2005: Advocacy group LGBT Human Rights Project GayRussia.Ru founded.

2006: Ryazan region passes a law against public acts or acts "aimed at promoting homosexuality among juveniles."

2008: Russian Ministry of Health ends ban on gay men giving blood.

2011: Arkhangelsk region passes its own ban on "gay propaganda" in the presence of minors.

Anti-gay attacker kicks a protester in Voronezh during a January 2013 demonstration against proposed national "gay propaganda" ban.

February 2012: Kostroma region passes a similar ban.

March 2012: St. Petersburg passes a similar ban.

May 2012: Seventeen people are arrested in St. Petersburg for displaying rainbow flags.

June 2012: Magadan region passes its own "gay propaganda" ban.

July 2012: Novosibirsk, Krasnodar and Samara regions pass similar bans.

August 2012: Bashkortostan region passes a similar ban, but without specifying any penalty or fine.

August 2012: Before giving a concert in St. Petersburg, pop singer Madonna states that she will not abide by the city's "gay propaganda" ban. She declares:

I'm a freedom fighter.
My show
My songs
My work
My art
Is all about freedom of expression
Freedom to choose to speak to act
Always with humanity and compassion
I will come to St. Petersburg to speak up for the gay community, to support the gay community and to give strength and inspiration to anyone who is or feels oppressed.
I don't run away from adversity.
I will speak during my show about this ridiculous atrocity.

August 2012: During her concert in St. Petersburg, Madonna criticizes the "gay propaganda" ban and tells fans that homosexuals should be treated with dignity and have the same rights as heterosexuals. She hands out pink bracelets to the audience to show solidarity with the city's gay and lesbian community.

August 2012: Anti-gay activists accuse Madonna of violating the "gay propaganda" ban and sue for $10.7 million in compensation for "moral damages."

August 2012: Moscow court upholds city decision to prohibit gay pride parades for the next 100 years.

November 2012: Court in St. Petersburg rules that Madonna did not break the law during her St. Petersburg concert. The judge notes that the concert tickets were labeled "18+" and orders the plaintiffs to pay concert organizers' legal costs.

December 2012: Prime Minister Dmitry Medvedev says laws about homosexuality are not needed.

December 2012: Pop singer Lady Gaga speaks up for gay rights during concerts in St. Petersburg and Moscow. She also thanks Medvedev for his opposition to a national "gay propaganda" ban. Opponents threaten legal action against her, but so far have not followed up on their threats.

December 2012: European Parliament calls on Russia to drop "gay propaganda" laws.

January 2013: Protests against proposed national "gay propaganda" law are held in Moscow, St. Petersburg, Voronezh, Arkhangelsk, Tomsk, Syktyvkar and Samara. Anti-gay attackers beat up protesters in Voronezh.

January 2013: Kaliningrad region adopts "gay propaganda" ban that applies whether children are present or not.

January 2013: On first reading, Russian State Duma votes overwhelmingly in favor of proposed national ban on "propaganda of homosexuality" in places where children might be present. The proposal, known as Article 6.13.1, is sent to committee for further discussion.

Ukraine:
'Read Oscar Wilde?
5 years in prison'

As the parliament in Ukraine considered imposing a ban on "gay propaganda" in early 2013, local gay rights activists launched a petition drive aimed at blocking it. To drum up support for the petition, they created ads that were displayed in Kiev metro stations.

The ads highlighted a provision that would impose prison sentences of three to five years for people whose actions could be considered endorsement of homosexuals:

"Read Oscar Wilde? Five years in prison."

"Listen to Queen? Five years in prison."

"Watch the films of Francois Ozon? Five years in prison."

The phrase translated here as "Five years (in prison)" is a double entendre. Its second meaning is a facetious reference to students' highest-ranked achievement — "Grade A."

"Read Oscar Wilde? Five years in prison."

The online petition invited people to register their opposition to the bill both because it would be a form of censorship and because it would violate people's right to information.

"I am against the government choosing for me which movies to watch, which books to read, and which opinions to express," the petition stated.

Jamaica:
Top 10 LGBT achievements
of 2012

Last year's top achievements affecting LGBT people in Jamaica were compiled by two activist groups, the Anti-Gay Fact Check and the Jamaica Forum for Lesbians, All-Sexuals & Gays (J-FLAG).

"2012 was another challenging year but there are a number of noteworthy achievements," they said. "Jamaicans—government and citizens—continue to show we are able to recognize and respect lesbian, gay, bisexual and transgender (LGBT) people, regardless of our differences."

About 20 percent of Jamaicans are supportive of LGBT people and their rights, according to two surveys.

"The 2012 Boxill Survey on Homophobia showed that one in five Jamaicans respects LGBT people. Additionally, one in five would support a Charter of Rights that includes sexual orientation as a ground for non-discrimination," the organizations stated.

These are the Top 10 achievements they cited for 2012:

FROM WRONGS TO GAY RIGHTS

1. Strong official response to a homophobic beating in November

"In an unprecedented move, the administration of the University of Technology (UTech) Jamaica has shown great leadership following the homophobic beating of an alleged gay student by other students and security guards on November 1, 2012.

"The university has undertaken a number of initiatives to address the matter, including the development of a plan of action for strengthening tolerance and respect for diversity among its various populations.

"It has held public discussions regarding tolerance and has developed diversity-training courses for security personnel to begin this year."

2. Official study of crimes against LGBTs

"The Ministry of National Security (MNS) has agreed to conduct a study on perceptions of safety and security within the LGBT community. The Ministry has expanded the 2013 Jamaica National Crime Victimization Survey (JNCVS) to include questions about crimes believed to result from assumptions about the sexual orientation of victims."

3. Improved relations between LGBT advocates and police

"J-FLAG continued to strengthen its relationship with the Jamaica Constabulary Force (JCF), including the Office of the Police Commissioner. This has led to an increase in LGBT persons reporting homophobic crimes and harassment to the police. The JCF has also named sexual orientation as a protected identity in the Police Ethics and Diversity Policy.

"Additionally, J-FLAG is part of a task force commissioned by the Police Commissioner to review issues within the St Andrew Central police division and identify and develop strategies to address them."

4. Some public support for improved security for LGBTs

"About a third of the population —— over 900,0000 Jamaicans —— believe the government is not doing enough to protect LGBT people from violence and discrimination."

FROM WRONGS TO GAY RIGHTS

5. Lawsuit over blocked TV ad seeking respect for LGBT people

"An unprecedented constitutional legal challenge launched by human rights lawyer Maurice Tomlinson of AIDS Free World against Television Jamaica, Public Broadcasting Corporation and CVM Television for their refusal to air an advertisement promoting the humanity of LGBT people. This is the first use of the new Charter of Rights and Fundamental Freedoms to access the media."

6. Progress in the entertainment industry

"Beenie Man (Moses David) in a very bold move apologised for anti-gay music he produced and performed in the past. Later in the year, international reggae artiste Diana King came out as Jamaica's first lesbian entertainer. To top it off LIME [a telecommunications company] canceled its school campaign with Potential Kidd as a result of a national outcry over lyrics which glorified and promoted sexual violence as better than being gay."

7. Improved access to health care

"Research by the Ministry of Health shows that more gay, bisexual and other men who have sex with men (MSM) are accessing health facilities for services related to HIV and other sexually transmitted infections. Twenty public health professionals from Kingston & St Andrew, St James and St Ann completed a nine-module capacity building training hosted by J-FLAG to better provide services to the LGBT community."

8. Public forum on homophobic bullying

"J-FLAG hosted its first public forum on homophobic bullying and human rights on May 17, 2012 at which the Minister of Education, Hon. Ronald Thwaites was the keynote speaker. Other government ministries were represented."

9. Health minister suggests changing the buggery law

"In December 2012, Minister of Health Hon. Dr. Fenton Ferguson highlighted at some events that the buggery law should be amended for

Jamaica to better facilitate the rights and development of LGBT Jamaicans." *[Editor's note: Under that law, anal intercourse is punishable by up to a 10-year prison sentence.]*

10. Expanded media coverage of LGBT issues

"Increased media output on human rights and LGBT issues, including the launch of Anti-Gay Fact Check, television and radio interviews. There were also a number of media exposes on the situation of homelessness among gay, bisexual and transgender Jamaicans."

The two groups said in summary:

> *"These achievements remind us that regardless of the colour of our skin, race, socio-economic status, sexual orientation, gender identity, geographical location and other priceless unique qualities that we are all one people — we are one Jamaica— and we can respect everyone.*

> *"This year let us endeavour to be even more respectful to each other. It is only with respect and embracing our common humanity that Jamaica can be a safe, cohesive and just society. Together, we can put aside the grievances that drive prejudice, inequality, crime, violence and intolerance. ...*

> *"As we continue to celebrate our 50th year of independence we must continue to be courageous and commit to rebuilding this great nation on the principles of mutual respect and equality as clearly articulated by our motto 'Out of Many, One People.' Gay or straight, Christian or non-Christian, Jamaica Labour Party or People's National Party, let us use our talents and resources to make Jamaica the place of choice to live, work, raise families and do business."*

Singapore:
Even hurting, let's win with love

Legal challenges to Singapore's law against gay sex have raised hopes for change, but also provoked harsh words from hard-line conservatives.

For example, megachurch pastor Lawrence Khang called the legal challenges "a looming threat" to social stability that would lead to the breakdown of the family and to attacks on freedom of religion and freedom of speech.

In response, a gay-rights coalition issued a statement of encouragement and consolation to Singapore's LGBT community and friends. It said:

"Recent events have caused much grief to many of us. Issues surrounding being LGBT are once again cast in the limelight and being discussed in the media.

"Hateful words have been used, disinformation has been spread as fact, and our leaders' positions do not appear to be evolving.

"While many of us are understandably hurt, even angered, by some insensitive comments that have been made, and there is fear that justice and equality may not prevail, it is important that we stay rational and keep calm.

"There will be little to be gained from responding to vitriol with more vitriol. In the words of Gandhi, 'Anger and intolerance are the enemies of correct understanding.'

"Let us not devolve into the very image of the angry and intolerant, whose hearts and minds we ought to win over through love and kindness."

SOURCES

FROM WRONGS TO GAY RIGHTS

Photo credits

COVER

Voronezh: Photo courtesy of Article20.org. **Uganda:** Photo by Rachel Adams.

OVERVIEWS

Victories, setbacks, close calls: 2012 in review

Photos courtesy of Facebook, official websites of Malawi and Jamaica, and Wikimedia Commons (Madonna photo by David Shankbone, Desmond Tutu photo by Remy Steinegger, copyright World Economic Forum)

78+ countries with anti-homosexuality laws

Data from 2012 report "State-Sponsored Homophobia: A World Survey of Laws Criminalising Same-Sex Sexual Acts Between Consenting Adults," published by the International Lesbian and Gay Association.

12 behind bars, 16 more awaiting trial on homosexuality charges

Photo of Jonas Singa Kumie, Franky Djome and Alice Nkom by Eric O. Lembembe. Photo of Roger Jean-Claude Mbede courtesy of Allout.org. Photo of Matthew Shepard courtesy of Wikipedia.

FROM WRONGS TO GAY RIGHTS

New activist network fights AIDS and anti-LGBT laws
Photo courtesy of St. Paul's Foundation for International Reconciliation.

Growing support for same-sex marriage
Data and quotations from multiple news reports.

What traditional African homosexuality learned from the West
Photos of Patrick Awondo and training session by Eric O. Lembembe. Photo of Mossi mask courtesy of Wikimedia Commons.

The fatal flaw in anti-AIDS strategies
Photo of Elly Ktabira courtesy of the International AIDS Society. Data on HIV rates from UNAIDS (2010), Baral, S. et al. (2008), Crane Survey Report (2010), Amfar (2008), and The Lancet (August 2009).

ISSUES OF FAITH

And the archbishop wondered: Dildos for the widows of Uganda?
Photo of Archbishop Yona Akoth courtesy of the Rev. Canon Albert Ogle.

Finding kindred spirits among straight allies in the faith community
Photo courtesy of the Rev. Canon Albert Ogle.

Bishop Christopher: Theological leper steps out in faith
Photos by Cary Bass via Wikimedia Commons and courtesy of the Rev. Canon Albert Ogle.

Homophobia: 'I too am infected'
Photo of George Regas courtesy of the Rev. Canon Albert Ogle. Photo of Gene Robinson by Donald Vish via Wikimedia Commons.

PERSONAL STORIES

A night in hell, Zimbabwe style
Photo of GALZ compound courtesy of GlobalGayz.com. Photo of Miles Tanhira courtesy of Miles Tanhira.

154

FROM WRONGS TO GAY RIGHTS

Gay in Cameroon: After beatings in prison, rejection at home
Photo of Roger Jean-Claude Mbede by Eric O. Lembembe.

Labeled effeminate because they drink Baileys, couple appeals 5-year sentence
Photos of Jonas Singa Kumie and Franky Djome courtesy of Amnesty International.

Meeting turns bloody as gay-bashers invade
Photo by Eric O. Lembembe.

Gay Pride Uganda
Photos by Rachel Adams.

For assaulted trans woman, Uganda medical care must be anonymous
Photos by Andy Kopsa.

HIV+ activist to Uganda: Stop impeding AIDS battle
Photo courtesy of Maxensia Nakibuuka via YouTube.

GLIMPSES

Russia: Timeline of gay rights and gay repression
Photo courtesy of Article20.org.

Ukraine: 'Read Oscar Wilde? 5 years in prison'
Photo courtesy of Insight.

About the authors

Rachel Adams is a documentary and portrait photographer based in the United Kingdom, who works with sub-cultures internationally, capturing otherwise unseen aspects of life.

Clare Byarugaba is co-coordinator of the Civil Society Coalition on Human Rights and Constitutional Law in Kampala, Uganda.

Andy Kopsa is a journalist based in New York City who writes about sex education, teen pregnancy, poverty and federal funding for anti-gay, anti-choice organizations.

The Rev. Canon Albert Ogle, an Episcopal priest, is founder and president of the St. Paul's Foundation for International Reconciliation, based in San Diego, California.

Eric O. Lembembe is a journalist in Yaoundé, Cameroon, and a leader of the Cameroonian Foundation for AIDS.

Colin Stewart is a 40-year journalism veteran and the editor/publisher of the Erasing 76 Crimes blog (http://76crimes.com), based in Laguna Niguel, California.

FROM WRONGS TO GAY RIGHTS

Miles Tanhira is a journalist, LGBTI rights activist, human rights defender, feminist and pacifist who formerly was head of information and communications for Gays and Lesbians of Zimbabwe.

17671612R00087

Made in the USA
Charleston, SC
22 February 2013